DIALOGUES

Stravinsky at Santa Fe, August 1963.

DIALOGUES

IGOR STRAVINSKY
and
ROBERT CRAFT

This edition first published in 2010
by Faber and Faber Ltd
Bloomsbury House, 74–77 Great Russell Street
London WC1B 3DA

Printed by Books on Demand GmbH, Norderstedt

All rights reserved
© Igor Stravinsky, 1961, 1962, 1963, 1968
© the Trust under the Will of Igor Stravinsky, 1982

The right of Igor Stravinsky and Robert Craft to be identified as authors
of this work has been asserted in accordance with Section 77 of the
Copyright, Designs and Patents Act 1988

This book is sold subject to the condition that it shall not, by way of
trade or otherwise, be lent, resold, hired out or otherwise circulated
without the publisher's prior consent in any form of binding or cover other than
that in which it is published and without a similar condition including this
condition being imposed on the subsequent purchaser

A CIP record for this book is available from the British Library

ISBN 978–0–571–25893–2

PUBLISHER'S NOTE

The fourth volume in the series of Stravinsky/Craft conversation books was originally published under the title *Dialogues and a Diary*. The present reissue contains the complete text of that volume with the exception of the final Diary section. This section, comprising extracts from a diary kept by Robert Craft while he accompanied Stravinsky on world-wide travels (1948–1962), is omitted since a more complete version of the diary is included in Robert Craft's book *Stravinsky: The Chronicle of a Friendship* (New York and London, 1972).

The other volumes in the series are:
Conversations with Igor Stravinsky
Memories and Commentaries
Expositions and Developments
Themes and Conclusions[1]

[1] The one-volume edition of *Themes and Episodes* (1966) and *Retrospectives and Conclusions* (1969) as revised by Igor Stravinsky in 1971.

ACKNOWLEDGMENTS

Grateful acknowledgment is made to the following publications in whose pages parts of this book have previously appeared: *Encounter, The Observer, Musical America, Mademoiselle, Show, HI FI-Stereo Review, Perspectives of New Music, Harper's, New York Review of Books, New York Times, Süddeutsche Zeitung, Commentary.*
The lines from *Exile and Other Poems, Seamarks* and *Winds*, by St.-John Perse, are reprinted by permission of Bollingen Foundation.
The photograph of Stravinsky at Santa Fe is by Claudio Spies, Stravinsky with Rex Harrison by courtesy of L. Arnold Weissberger and Stravinsky with Boulez by Daniel Cande.

CONTENTS

INTRODUCTION: A Master at Work	*page* 13
A GREEK TRILOGY	
Oedipus Rex	21
Apollo	32
Perséphone	36
PROGRAMME NOTES	
Octuor	39
Four-hand Piano Music	40
Symphony of Psalms	44
Violin Concerto	47
Scènes de Ballet	48
Symphony in Three Movements	50
Jazz Commercials	52
INTERVIEWS	
The Musical Scene and Other Matters	55
Music and the Statistical Age	63
WORKING NOTES FOR *The Flood*	72
STRAVINSKY REVIEWS *The Rite*	81
SOME PEOPLE	
Writers	91
Composers	99
Some Older Composers	112

PERSONAL
    Contemporary Music and Recording   119
    Thoughts of an Octogenarian   123

APPENDICES   131

LETTERS ON 'OEDIPUS REX' (1925–27)   135

    Index of Works by Stravinsky   145
    Index of People and Places   147

ILLUSTRATIONS

    Stravinsky at Santa Fe, August 1963.   Frontispiece

1. Stravinsky's father's grave in Leningrad,
   photographed in 1925.   *facing page* 54

2. With Prokofiev and Ernest Ansermet,
   Talloires, 1929.   55

3. With Ramuz, 1932.   55

4. Stravinsky with his son Soulima, on the *Cap
   Arcona*, June 16, 1936.   80

5. Two photographs of the Düsseldorf Exhibition
   of Decadent Music, 1938   81

6. With Pierre Boulez, Paris, May, 1962.   118

7. With Rex Harrison, New York, 1964.   119

    Draft by Cocteau for *Oedipus Rex*   136–7

INTRODUCTION
ROBERT CRAFT

A Master at Work[1]

Stravinsky again! (still? yet?): eighty-four last week, but still composing, still speaking his mind, still vital. It is precisely this actuality that distinguishes the festival of his music at the Philharmonic next month. Homage on such a scale is rarely accorded an active contemporary, for the reason that most artists at the homage-receiving time of life are still stranded in the period of their first flowering, and hence have ceased to *be* contemporary. Moreover, few contemporary artists of any age have produced a variety of work rich enough to sustain an active exhibition of this sort, rather than a museum retrospective. But Stravinsky qualifies; he is one of the representative spokesmen of 1966 as he was of 1906, '16, '26, and so on. And for practical-minded programme-builders he qualifies richly on other grounds as well. No one has illuminated larger areas of the past, or of the present in the past, and at the same time left so deep an imprint on so many successors, apostolic and otherwise. Stravinsky as a point of intersection is as much the theme of the festival as Stravinsky's music.

That the more permanent part of his activity takes place in Hollywood must be well known, the contents of his studio there having been televised, still-photographed, described in tyrianthine prose. But the changes of recent years have not been recorded by any of these media. The room is air-conditioned now, and often reduced to what seems like near frostbite temperature, a surprising difference to friends who remember the composer's former valetudinarianism, and his apprehensions of the slightest draught or breath of cool air; the transformation is due to a blood disease which overheats him. Another difference is in the display of honours: the mounted shofar from Israel; the silver-framed benison from the Pope; the Grand Cross of Santiago from Portugal;

[1] *N.Y. Times*, June 19, 1966.

the Dresden ware from the Bürgermeister of Berlin and the first edition of Lessing from the Bürgermeister of Hamburg; the 'keys' to American cities and the plaques, scrolls, medals from foreign ones; trophies such as these did not exist a few years ago and would not have been exposed if they had. But there is another change that I think most likely to impress the visitor. This is the presence of so many reminders of death: the portraits of the composer by the late Giacometti, the photographs of Pope John, President Kennedy, T. S. Eliot, Cocteau, Aldous Huxley, Evelyn Waugh, and of Celeste, Stravinsky's beloved cat. Eight of the composer's later pieces bear the subtitle 'In Memoriam.'

Stravinsky still composes at the piano but not exclusively, at least not in the preliminary stages. Music paper, or styluses and unlined paper, are close to hand on all of his peregrinations, and he seems to be visited with a great deal of what may or may not be inspiration on airplanes; perhaps the perfect composing conditions for him would be found on an interplanetary flight. Any scrap of paper—bit of an envelope, back of a menu or programme, napkin, margin torn from a magazine—will do for notations, which is why the pages of the notebooks in which these sketches are pasted look like collages. Stravinsky dates each sketch and marks each choice of serial route in coloured pencils, for the simple reason, he says, that it is otherwise so difficult to check errors, though obviously it is more than that; in fact the manifestation of a powerful compulsion for order.

Stravinsky's compositional procedures seem not to have changed in late years. He almost always begins with a melodic idea, which in the first writing may be expressed only by its rhythmic values. He will often compose this single line, in isolation it seems, to a point where larger shapes become clear to him. The piano is not resorted to in this melody-forging stage, but only when harmonic and contrapuntal ideas begin to appear; it is then that Stravinsky will say he has invented (*i.e.*, discovered) something which he now intends to compose (*i.e.*, develop). Inventing usually seems to occur in the mornings, and most intensively toward noon, whereas composition is largely post-meridional; at present Stravinsky leaves his rooms before lunch only for a walk, a forbiddingly solitary exercise more for mind-limbering, than as his doctors have ordered, limb-minding. There are no fixed hours for the work of instrumentation. As soon as a substantial unit has been completed in sketch score he will work overtime to finish the orchestra score: this goes at high speed, or, rather, as fast as it is possible to write on transparencies, for he does not use Xerox or a music typewriter. It is a function of the composer's daughter (another is trimming her father's hair) to arrange for the reproduction of these scores, and to post them to the publisher, sometimes virtually page by page, for Stravinsky never looks back, as though he were afraid his Eurydice might disappear. His daughter is the custodian of all manuscripts of work-in-progress during her father's absences.

Stravinsky's work extends to more than composing, as record-buyers, book-review readers, concert-goers, and TV-viewers hardly need to be told. As he did not lack advocates among performers, and as he was over forty when he began to conduct, the financial motive he himself gives for this new career may be accepted, at least in part. Not being able to live on the income from his compositions, he became a summer composer—concert life being much less developed in that season then than now—and a whistle-stop guest-conductor and touring recitalist in winter. In late years the number of concert appearances has fallen to very few, but they continue nevertheless, and avowedly for the same reason, though the real one is simply the unrenounceable love of live music-making. The forty-year habit seems impossible to arrest entirely, in fact, and the stimulation and pleasure to *him* (at least) from conducting seem visibly to sustain his age.

For a backstage glimpse of Stravinsky on tour I shall try to photograph him as he is at this moment in his hotel room, in Paris, where he is reposing before a series of concerts; or, rather, since he dislikes being photographed, I shall attempt to snapshoot the room itself: it says a great deal about the man. Within a half-hour of occupancy its character was entirely transformed. The medicines, toiletries, and sacred images neatly set out on the bed-table; the clothes tidily piled in dressers and hung in closets; the immaculate arrangement of writing materials, business papers, letter files, dictionaries and other books: all of these exemplify Stravinskian order. The composer's individuating touch is also reflected in his replacement of the 'Utrillo' and the 'Van Gogh' with pictures from magazines which he has scotch-taped to the wall; and in the pile of extra pillows on his bed; and the green beret on the pillows, for he sleeps in this *aficionado's* headgear as if it were an eighteenth-century night cap. The files are extensive and as space-consuming as the books, which fill a small shelf. His daily tally of the economy will include such minute investments as the purchase of a postage stamp, and the medical book-keeping is even more thorough. The weekly blood-tests are recorded together with a schedule of syndrome and other anticoagulants that is literally the composer's lifeline. The copious correspondence does not go untended during concert tours, either, and though the composer's pen pals may reasonably be suspected of collectors' interests in their in-mail, he is rarely the party in arrears. Stravinsky, on the road, is his own clipping service, too; articles on science, art, archeology, books are painstakingly scissored out and sorted away, often with initialled comment. But it is disturbing to discover obituaries pasted in the very sketch-book calendar of his present work (photographs of Scherchen and Jean Arp were entered there only last week); disturbing to see that death is not only in the composer's thoughts but close to his creative ones as well. He appeared at breakfast a few mornings ago saying, 'I dreamed I could walk normally again and saw myself in a crowd keeping pace with everybody else. It was cruel to wake up.'

Stravinsky, the gourmet, is always happy in Paris, though in his favourite restaurants, Ami Louis (the world capital of *foie gras*), the Boule d'Or, the Grand Véfour, the delights of the table are dangerously good. As I write, in fact, the great composer's liver is giving him complaint. And no wonder. After unpacking, he sped to one of these restaurants, ostensibly for its view of an old *quartier*, but he was soon seated and consuming crayfish (irresistible to Russians) at an alarming rate. He himself does not attribute his discomfort to gross quantity, however, and his own diagnosis rests on a far nicer point. As he had been shown the delectable monsters in the kitchen still in the quick he now thinks he is being punished for betraying them and for the sin of 'eating creatures that one has already met socially.' In truth, though, at eighty-four Stravinsky still has some of the appetites of a Pantagruel.

But let us return to the scene of that more permanent work achieved principally in California. On a good day Stravinsky still manages to devote four or five hours to composition, and more than that on week-ends when there are fewer interruptions from telephones—which can be expected to split through thoughts and feelings about thirty times a day, normally, and on eight resonant extensions. And there are other rackets: a piano-practising neighbour, very conscientious at scales; and another, equally dutiful with a bugle and set of 'traps'; and birds, as dependably melodious at night as the Hi-Fi canaries at Forest Lawn; and ear-piercing smog-warning sirens (or are they Viet Cong warnings?); and helicopters, for whom the Stravinsky residence appears to be an important marker on an aerial freeway. As no one could be more sensitive to these auditory tortures than the composer—he still flinches at any noise a full second faster than anyone else—it is a marvel that he can work at all.

The composer's entertainments are unexceptional. Reading is the most important; he reads as much as a book reviewer and in range from the classics to the airmail editions of several foreign weeklies. He rarely braves the cinema any more, but will turn on the 'telly' sooner than you can say 'Jackie Gleason' (and turn it off even sooner). Diversion is afforded by the gardens, both flower and fruit. The composer takes great pride in, and pretends to prefer, the lemons, oranges, and avocados from his own trees. He is fond of animals, too, and even of the lizards which, in warm weather, slither over his preserves; I might add that the lacertilian lullabies of that musical species frequenting bedroom walls in the Philippines enchanted him on his visit there, as they horrified me. He also relishes cruising about in one of his (two) Continentals, though only when Madame Stravinsky is at the wheel, for then it is possible to enjoy some backseat driving.

If I were asked which people share comparatively easy access to Stravinsky at present, I would have to say that Russian-speaking visitors are greatly favoured, and that time will be found for a Magaloff, a Joel Spiegelman, a Ussachevsky, a Hurok, an Isaac Stern, a Babin and a Vronsky when it will be denied to others; nowadays it is a relaxation for Stravinsky simply to converse in his mother tongue. He has begun to open his doors to historians, too, when their quests have tended to concentrate on his associates and concern himself only indirectly. Not long ago he promised to contribute to a BBC television documentary about Diaghilev, and he has recently entrusted his Cocteau material to Francis Steegmuller, whose biographies of Flaubert and Maupassant he admires. But of the old circle of really intimate friends, few survive.

Have the tempers of the man and his music changed in recent years? The chemical balances are different, in any case, but more than that it is hard to say. Stravinsky was and is an essentially happy spirit. The majority of his compositions can be described as *divertimenti*, whereas the emotion of only a handful could be called tragic. His most profound moods (not the same as his most profound music) are generally found in his religious works, and it is there, too, that the chemistry shift is most noticeable: Stravinsky seems to be more exclusively a religious composer now than before. At the same time, the moods of all of his music, the barbaric exuberance, the joking and leg-pulling (there is a fat Rossini imprisoned in this thin man), the exaltation, the anger, the serenity (*Apollo*), the gentleness (the lullaby in *Perséphone*): these cross the boundaries and are discovered in all of his forms. They are expressions of a humanity that has informed not only the musical sensibilities of our age but also its minds and hearts.

Dialogues

A GREEK TRILOGY

Oedipus Rex

R.C.: What do you recall of the circumstances that led to the composition of *Oedipus Rex*? To what extent did you collaborate with Cocteau on the scenario and the text? What was your purpose in translating the libretto into Latin, and why Latin rather than Greek—or, if Latin, then why not directly from Greek? What were your original ideas for staging the work and why have they never been realized? What did you mean by opera-oratorio? How would you identify the religious character of the work, if you agree with those people who profess to hear religious elements in it? Would you discuss what you call the musical manners of the piece? And, what more can you contribute to performance knowledge, and to the history of the work in performance?

I.S.: I date the beginnings of my *Oedipus Rex* from September 1925, but at least five years earlier than that I had been aware of the need to compose a large-scale dramatic work. Returning from Venice to Nice that September, I stopped in Genoa to renew memories of the city in which I had spent my fifth wedding anniversary, in 1911. There, in a bookstall I saw a life of Francis of Assisi which I bought and, that night, read. To this reading I owe the formulation of an idea that had occurred to me often, though vaguely, since I had become *déraciné*. The idea was that a text for music might be endowed with a certain monumental character by translation backwards, so to speak, from a secular to a sacred language. 'Sacred' might mean no more than 'older', as one could say that the language of the King James Bible is more sacred than the language of the New English Bible, if only because of its greater age. But I thought that an older, even an imperfectly remembered, language must contain an incantatory element that could be exploited in music. The confirming example from Francis of Assisi was that of the Saint's hieratic use of Provençal, the poetic language of the renaissance of the Rhône, in contrast to his quotidian Italian, or Brass Age Latin. Prior to that moment of illumination in Genoa, I was unable to resolve the language problem in my future vocal works. Russian, the exiled language of my heart, had become musically impracticable, and French, German, and Italian were temperamentally alien. When I work with words in music, my musical saliva is set in motion by the sounds and rhythms of the syllables, and 'In the beginning was the word' is, for me, a literal, localized truth. But the problem was resolved, and the search for '*un pur langage sans office*' (St.-John Perse) ended with my rediscovery of Ciceronian Latin.

The decision to compose a work on the play by Sophocles followed quickly upon my return to Nice, but the choice was preordained. I wanted a universal plot or, at least, one so well known that I would not have to elaborate its exposition. I wished to leave the play, as play, behind, thinking by this to distil the dramatic essence and to free myself for a greater degree of focus on a purely musical dramatization. Various Greek myths came to mind as I considered subjects, and then, almost in automatic succession, I thought of the play that I had loved most in my youth. In a final moment of doubt I reconsidered the possibility of using a modern language version of one of the myths, but only *Phèdre* fulfilled my conception of the statuesque, and what musician could breathe in that metre?

I invited Cocteau's collaboration* because I greatly admired his *Antigone*. I told him my ideas and cautioned him that I did not want an action drama, but a 'still life.' I also said that I wanted a conventional libretto with arias and recitatives, though the conventional, I knew, was not his strongest suit. He appeared to be enthusiastic about the project except for the notion that his phrases were to be recast in Latin, but the first draft of his libretto was precisely what I did not want: a music drama in meretricious prose.

'Music drama' and 'opera' have long since blurred together, of course, but they were firm categories in my mind at that time, and I even used to argue such extenuating notions as that the orchestra has a larger and more exterior interpretative role in 'music drama.' I would now replace these terms by 'verse opera' and 'prose opera,' identifying the new categories with such pure examples as *The Rake's Progress* for the type of the former and

* See 'Letters on *Oedipus Rex*', pp. 135-44.

Erwartung for the type of the latter. Divisions of this sort, no matter how factitious, are necessary to my forming processes.

Cocteau was more than patient with me and my criticisms. The whole book was rewritten twice, and even after that he submitted it to a final shearing. (I am a topiarist at heart, and my love for clipping things sometimes amounts to a mania.) What is purely Cocteau's in the libretto? I am no longer able to say, but I should think less the shape of it than the gesticulation of the phrasing. (I do not refer to the practice of repeating words, which is habitual with me and which dates only from the time when I begin to compose.) The speaker device is Cocteau's and the notion that the speaker should wear a *frac* and comport himself like a *conférencier* (which has too often meant, in practice, like a master of ceremonies). But music goes beyond words, and the music was inspired by the tragedy of Sophocles.

I had begun to visualize the staging as soon as I started to compose the music. I saw the chorus first, seating in a single row across the stage and reaching from end to end of the proscenium rainbow. I thought that the singers should seem to read from scrolls, and that only these scrolls and the outlines of their bearers' cowled heads should be seen. My first and strongest conviction was that the chorus should not have a face.

My second idea was that the actors should stand on pedestals and wear cothurni, each person at a different height, behind the chorus. But actors is the wrong word. No one 'acts,' and the only individual who moves at all is the narrator, and he merely to show his detachment from the other stage figures. *Oedipus Rex* may or may not be an opera by virtue of its musical content, but it is not at all operatic in the sense of movement. The people in the play relate to each other not by gestures, but by words. They do not turn to listen to each other's speeches, but address themselves directly to the audience. I thought that they should stand rigidly, and in my original version I did not even allow them exits and entrances. My first conception was that the people of the play should be revealed from behind small individual curtains, but I realized later that the same effect might be accomplished more easily by lighting. Like the Commendatore, the singers should be illuminated during their arias and become vocally, though not physically, galvanized statues. Oedipus himself should stand in full view throughout, of course, except after the '*Lux facta est*,' when he must change masks.

(He could be recountenanced behind his individual curtain or in the dark.) His self-violence is described, but not enacted: he should not move. Those directors who whisk him offstage and then bring him back realistically staggering in an unreal, stylized, costume have understood nothing of my music.

I am often asked why I should have tried to compose a wax-works opera. My answer has been that I abhor *verismo*, but a complete reply would be more positive and more complex. For one thing, I consider this static representation a more vital way to focus the tragedy not on Oedipus himself and the other individuals, but on the 'fatal development' that, for me, is the meaning of the play. Oedipus, the man, is a subject for a type of symbolic treatment which depends upon the interpretation of experience and is principally psychological. This did not attract me as musical material, and if it had, I would have constructed the drama differently—for example, by adding a scene from the childhood of the prince. My audience is not indifferent to the fate of the person, but I think it far more concerned with the person of the fate and the delineation of it which can be achieved uniquely in music. But so far as visualization may give support, the stage figures are more dramatically isolated and helpless precisely because they are plastically mute, and the portrait of the individual as the victim of circumstances is made far more starkly effective by this static presentation. Crossroads are not personal but geometrical, and the geometry of tragedy, the inevitable intersecting of lines, is what concerned me.

I have also been asked why I failed to take one more step and use puppets, as my late friend Robert Edmond Jones once did for a performance of my *Oedipus* in New York. This notion did occur to me, in fact, and I had been impressed by Gordon Craig's puppets when he showed them to me in Rome in 1917. But I am also fond of masks, and while composing Oedipus' first aria I already imagined him wearing a roseate, ogival one, like that of a Chinese sun-god—just as, when I composed the Devil's music in *The Flood*, I imagined a singer made to seem transparent, like a scorpion.

My staging ideas[1] were not realized simply because Diaghilev lacked time to mount the work at its première; and because the first performance was unstaged, many people assumed that I preferred the work to be given that way. *Oedipus Rex* was composed as a twentieth-anniversary present for the Diaghilev Ballet—'*Un*

[1] The *Avant-propos* in the score only partly represents them.

cadeau très macabre,' Diaghilev called it. Its existence was kept secret from him until the last moment, and I was late in finishing the score, so late that the singers hardly had learned the notes before the piano preview performance, which took place at Edmond de Polignac's a few days before the public one. At this Polignac soirée I accompanied the singers myself, and from the reactions of the guests I foresaw that *Oedipus* was not likely to succeed with the Parisian ballet audience. But my austere vocal concert, following a very colourful ballet, was an even greater failure than I had anticipated. The audience was hardly more than polite, and the Sganarelles of the press were a lot less than that: '*Celui qui a composé Pétrouchka nous présente avec cette pastiche Handelienne ... Un tas de gens mal habillés ont mal chanté ... La musique de Créon est une marche Meyerbeerienne*,' etc. Performances were rare in the next two decades, but since then they have been more and more frequent.

I should note that Diaghilev himself was cool to *Oedipus* at the première, but I think that this may have been because of Cocteau. A very handsome, very young man was deliberately chosen to be the speaker, at any rate, and this was certainly to spite Cocteau, who, when composing the play, must have thought of that part for himself.

I have participated as a conductor in only a few staged performances, and I have seen few other stagings. (Of recent ones I should mention the Vienna Opera's, where the '*e peste*' sounded as though the singers really did have the plague, and the Washington Opera's, where the white faces of the chorus glistened from rectangular towers like holes in Emmentaler cheese.) The performance that has pleased me most, visually, was Cocteau's in the Théâtre des Champs Elysées, in May 1952. His huge masks were very striking, and so, though it contradicted my idea, was his use of symbolic mime. I wince when I recall the first staged performances, in the Kroll Opera, Berlin, though they were musically well prepared by Otto Klemperer. The speaker wore a black pierrot costume. I complained to the director that this did not seem relevant to the *Oedipus* story, but his answer permitted no further argument: 'Herr Professor Strawinsky, in our country only the *Kapellmeister* is allowed to wear a *Frack*.' Hindemith and Schoenberg were in the audience at the Berlin performance, the former *hingerissen*, and the latter—who must have heard in it nothing but empty *ostinato* patterns and primitive harmonies—*abgekühlt*.

In what sense is the music religious? I do not know how to answer because the word does not correspond in my mind to states of feeling or sentiment, but to dogmatic beliefs. A Christianized *Oedipus* would require the truth-finding process to resemble an *auto-da-fé*, and I had no interest in attempting that. I can testify that the music was composed during my strictest and most earnest period of Christian Orthodoxy. At the beginning of September 1925, with a suppurating abscess in my right forefinger, I left Nice to perform my Piano Sonata in Venice. I had prayed in a little church near Nice, before an old and 'miraculous' icon, but I expected that the concert would have to be cancelled. My finger was still festering when I walked on to the stage at the Teatro La Fenice, and I addressed the audience, apologizing in advance for what would have to be a poor performance. I sat down, removed the little bandage, felt that the pain had suddenly stopped, and discovered that the finger was—miraculously, it seemed to me—healed. (Now I grant that minor 'miracles' are more disconcerting than even the most far-fetched 'psychosomatic' rationale, and the reader who has come this far will probably decide that all I had was a *maladie imaginaire*. But a miracle is what seemed to have happened to me and if it was no such thing, and another word is used to describe it, then the fact that I took it for a miracle is at least as significant to the reader. I do, of course, believe in a system beyond Nature.)

A few days after this Venetian concert, I discovered the book about St. Francis and decided after reading it to use the language that is also the language of the Western Church, and shortly after that I chose the archetypal drama of purification. I also composed a Russian liturgical-style *Pater Noster* at the same time as *Oedipus Rex*, and I was certainly influenced in composing the '*Gloria*' chorus by Russian Church ritual: the Holy Trinity is symbolized by the triple repetitions, just as it is in the *Kyrie* of the Mass. But, to begin with, the character of the '*Gloria*' music itself is ecclesiastical.

Although I have been concerned with questions of musical manners all my life, I am unable to say precisely what these manners are. That, I think, is because they are not precompositional, but of the essence of the musical act: the manner of saying and the thing said are, for me, the same. But am I not unusually conscious of the manner question, nevertheless? All I can say is that my manners are my personal relations with my material. *Je me rends compte* in them. Through them I discover my laws. The direction of the next melodic interval is involved with the musical manners of the whole work. Thus, the clarinet trill at '*lux facta est*' is a manifestation of my *Oedipus* manners: the trill is not just a trill but an indispensable mannerism. I have been told that such things merely indicate the culture-consciousness found in all *emigrés*,[2] but I know that the explanation is deeper than that, as I worked and thought in exactly the same way in Russia. My manners are the birthmark of my art.

I began to compose according to a plan of gradation for the musicodramatic development, a recitative–aria scheme in which each aria was to mark a crucial development in the story. My first idea was that each dramatic progression was to be accompanied by a downward pull of the key-centre, somewhat in the tradition of the baroque composers, though in saying this I must quickly add that I did not refer to any models. I do not now recall any predatory attractions to other composers at the time, though, if another composer is suggested in my score, he is Verdi. Much of the music is a *Merzbild*, put together from whatever came to hand. I mean, for example, such little games as the offbeats at No. 50 and the Alberti-bass horn solo accompanying the Messenger. I also mean the fusion of such widely divergent types of music as the *Folies Bergères* tune at No. 40 ('The girls enter, kicking') and the Wagnerian 7th-chords at Nos. 58 and 74. I have made these bits and snatches my own, I think, and of them a unity. 'Soule is form,' Spenser says, 'and doth the bodie make.' (And I would apply that quotation to *Le Baiser de la fée* as well. Listening the other day to a concert of the saccharine source material for that work, I almost succumbed to diabetes.)

What were my first musical ideas for *Oedipus*? Well, what *are* musical ideas? An idea is already a formulation, is it not, and does not something happen before that? I, at any rate, am aware of a precognitive sense of my material long before I have any notion of

---

[2] And I am a double *emigré*, born to a minor musical tradition and twice transplanted to other minor ones. I myself, and not political circumstance or the Revolution, helped to exhaust and scuttle the limited tradition of my birthright, but the dead end of 'Russian music' was the reason for my removal to 'French music,' which, at the time, was almost as eclectic as 'Russian music' and even less 'traditional.' My second removal was to America.

how to use it. I know also that this material cannot be imposed upon by 'ideas,' but that something very like the contrary takes place.[3] All of my 'ideas' for *Oedipus Rex* were in one sense derived from what I call the versification—though by 'ideas' I may mean nothing more than what I have already described as manners.[4] And what do I mean by 'versification'? I can answer only by saying that at present I make my 'versification' with series as an artist of another kind may versify with angles or numbers.

The *Oedipus* music was composed from beginning to end in the order in which it now stands. I was not conscious of the manner question as I composed the first chorus, and when I did begin to understand it, in Oedipus' aria, I may have established it too exaggeratedly, which is to say, too conventionally. This, I think, was because I realized that it would have to be fixed then and there for the whole work. The King's manner conceals the King's 'heart,' though not, perhaps, the tail feathers of his pride.

I frame the word heart with diacritical marks because I do not believe the Greeks would have used it in our sense or, at least, with our emphasis, and even if they did temperamentalize it, they were careful to balance it in their cosmogony of affective organs by the *hepar*. (The Greeks must have divined that the liver is a regenerative organ, incidentally, though medical science has only recently determined the fact, for otherwise Prometheus' punishment would have had no retributive meaning—the birds would have had of him no more than an *hors d'oeuvre*.) But whereas journalists may claim utility for 'heart' and 'heartless,' 'cold,' the key word in most attacks on *Oedipus*, is propaganda, verbicide through the wish to evaluate rather than to describe. What is 'warm,' please? *Schmaltz*? And is the first canon in the Goldberg Variations cold or warm?

Criticism should seek to discover the effect produced by the fact that the harmonic dominant is so often in the minor. It should also analyse the nature of the music's rhythmic manners, the hint for

---

[3] Composition begins when some one thing preponderates over another, a statement I cannot elucidate because my outer mind is a better superintendent than observer of my inner mind and because I am overwary of concepts that I suspect of being word mirrors and no more.

[4] One's forms are a stamp of oneself, of one's physical, bilateral apprehension of experience, and form and function are the same.

which came from Sophocles himself or, more precisely, from the metres of the chorus (especially the simple choriambics, the anapaests and dactyls rather than the glyconics and dochmii). No one seems to have noticed that where Sophocles has used what may be called a 3/8 rhythm I have used the 6/8, and that just as his chorus sings of the gods in 4/4 dactyls, my Créon, who is on the side of the gods, sings in the same metre. And, in general, I exploit rhythmic staticity in the same way as Sophocles. Listen, for example, to the choral passage in his play just before the appearance of the Shepherd. The rhythms in *Oedipus* are more static and regular than in any other composition of mine to that date, and the tension created by them in the '*Mulier in vestibulo*' chorus, for instance, is greater than any tension that irregular, upset rhythms could produce. But precisely that chorus—I call it a mortuary *tarantella*—has been cited as a piece of inappropriate gaiety, a ballet coda, even as a cancan—by people who have no manners of their own. The rhythms are the principal source of dramatic tension and a major element of the dramatic method. If I have succeeded in freezing the drama in the music, that was accomplished largely by rhythmic means.

My musical performance notes are few. I repeat the '*Gloria*' chorus after the narrator's speech both because I like the chorus and because I prefer to go directly, without narration, from *tutti* G major to *solo* flute and harp G minor. And in stage performances I like to acknowledge the audience's realization that the Queen Mother must have a lot to say by giving them a pause before she says it. I should mention, too, that I prefer the 1948 version of the score. The revisions are not mere copyright changes, but improvements instituted in my manuscript immediately following the first performance. I refer to such things as the added horns and tuba in the '*Aspikite*' chorus, and the added trumpet in the 'Beckmesser' aria, '*Nonne Monstrum*'. I would also advise conductors that the part of Oedipus himself should not be sung by a large operatic voice, but by a lyrical one. The Oedipus singer must exploit dynamic contrasts, and his gradations in volume are extremely important. The first aria, for example, must be quiet, not bellowed, and the melismata must be given strict and full rhythmic value.

My criticisms of *Oedipus Rex*? Criticism is too easy after thirty-five years, and, what is worse, too late, but I detest the speaker device, that disturbing series of interruptions, and I do not much like the speeches themselves. '*Il tombe, il tombe de haut*'—from where else, indeed, given the gravity situation? (The English is not much better, though: 'He falls headlong' sounds like the description of a swan dive.) The line 'And now you will hear the famous monologue, "the Divine Iokaste is dead,"' is intolerable snobbery. Famous to whom? And no monologue follows, but only a fourword singing telegram. Another line mentions a 'witness to the murder, who steps from the shadows,' and I have always wondered who that interesting character might be and what might have become of him. But the final '*on t'aimait*' is the most offensive phrase of all, for it is a journalist's caption and a blot of sentimentality wholly alien to the manners of the work. But alas, the music was composed with the speeches, and is paced by them.

The music? I love it, all of it, even the Messenger's fanfares, which remind me of the now badly tarnished trumpets of early 20th-Century-Fox. Neoclassicism? A husk of style? Cultured pearls? Well, which of us today is not a highly conditioned oyster? I know that the *Oedipus* music is valued at about zero by present progressive-evolutionary standards, but I think it may last awhile in spite of that. I know, too, that I relate only from an angle to the German stem (Bach—Haydn—Mozart—Beethoven—Schubert—Brahms—Wagner—Mahler—Schoenberg), which evaluates largely in terms of where a thing comes from and where it is going. But an angle may be an advantage.

R.C.: Did you choose Jean Daniélou to make the Latin translation of *Oedipus*? Would you comment on his work?

I.S.: Daniélou was a friend of Cocteau. I did not know him, and in fact we have never met. He was attached to a monastic order in India then, or so I think, but I may be confusing him with his brother Alain, the orientalist and musicologist. Jean Daniélou eventually became a priest, in any case, and an author of books on patristic typology, especially the *Sacramentum Futuri* (Paris, 1950), which contains an absorbing study of Philo and Alexandrian Judaism. His only work in English that I know is an essay on Gregory of Nyssa.

I used Latin rather than Greek, to answer your earlier question, because I had no notion of how to treat Greek musically (or Latin, Latinists will say, but there I did at least have *my* idea). I sometimes read in programme notes that the language of my *Oedipus* is 'medieval Latin,' a rumour no doubt derived from the fact that the translator was a Catholic cleric. But the Latin, judging by the sentence structure, the placement of modifiers, and the use of the historical infinitive, is Ciceronian. I have found only one 'ecclesiastical' word in the whole libretto, and that—the *omniscius pastor*—can be called such only by association. (*Why* the shepherd should be omniscient I do not know.) Unusual grammatical constructions can be found—for example, the ablative form '*Laudibus Regina*'—which Daniélou may have borrowed from an old text—but they are rare. Idiomatically, the language is all pre-Boethian. But the Latinist is already horrified by the first letter of my score, the 'K', which does not exist in the language he knows. The purpose of this barbarian orthography was to secure hard, or at least non-Italianized, sounds instead of the usual potpourri of classic and ecclesiastic. I have misspelled a word, too, because of an error in transliteration from Russian: '*Miki*,' at rehearsal number 50, is a mistake for '*Mihi*.'

'Stravinsky's scansion of the Latin syllables is sometimes rather unorthodox.' I quote a much quoted criticism. In fact, my scansion is entirely unorthodox. It must break every rule, if only because Latin is a language of fixed accents and I accentuate freely according to my musical dictates. Even the shift from '*OE*dipus' (which should be pronounced '*OY*dipus' by the singers and '*EE*dipus' by the speaker[5]) to 'Oe*DI*pus' is unthinkable from the point of view of speech, which, of course, is *not* my point of view.

I have noted in my own score that '*Vale*' should be '*Ave*' in the salute to Créon, as to say 'good-bye' at this point would be an incongruous intrusion of low comedy; that the grammar, and therefore the meaning,[6] is obscure in the passage from '*Non reperias*' to '*istum pellere*,' and that later in this same speech the construction '*Polliceor divinabo*'—'I promise,' or 'I shall guess'—is freakish; that '*accusat*' and '*accusas*' in the Oedipus–Tiresias exchange are misspelled; that the string of plosive consonants in Tiresias' '*Dicam, dicam quod dixit deus*' is good sound but bad Latin, though for this I claim musical licence; that the accent shift on the last syllable of each of the final '*Glorias*'—in the salute to the Queen—should be avoided by exaggerating the tonic accent; that '*Mentiantur*,' in

[5] The 'pus' must rhyme with moose, 'Tiresias' must be pronounced 'Tyreesias,' and Jocasta in three syllables—'Iokaste.'
[6] I no longer possess a copy of the French text, and I can only guess at the original meaning.

Iokaste's aria, is a printer's error, but a grave one: the Queen is supposed to say 'They lie'—'Ment*iun*tur'—not 'they may lie'; that '*Oedipoda*' is an unusual form and should perhaps be changed to '*Oedipodem*' or '*Oedipum*.'

Apollo

R.C.: What do you recall of the genesis of your *Apollo*, the circumstances of the commission, the choice of subject, the career of the work in performance? Was the idea to imitate Alexandrines melodically—you once referred to *Apollo* as an exercise in iambics—your first musical idea? Your own performances of *Apollo* differ rhythmically from the printed score in many ways. Would you comment on these corrections, if that is what they are?

I.S.: *Apollo* was commissioned by Elizabeth Sprague Coolidge for performance in the Library of Congress. Or, more precisely, Mrs. Coolidge asked for a work of thirty minutes' duration—a condition I satisfied with the exactitude of a film composer—employing an instrumentation appropriate to a small hall. The choice of the subject and the choice of the string ensemble were my own.

Diaghilev was very annoyed when he learned that I had composed a ballet for someone else, and though he acquired it gratis after the Washington première, he never forgave my (as he thought) disloyalty:

> '*Cette Américaine est complètement sourde.*'
> '*Elle est sourde, mais elle paie.*'
> '*Tu penses toujours à l'argent.*'

The '*argent*,' though, was only one thousand dollars. My monetary discussions with Diaghilev were always the same and always unresolvable. What he called stinginess I called economy. I was never wildly dispendious, to be sure, though neither was my only goal the promise of numismatic bliss, as Diaghilev pretended. (Diaghilev also used to pretend that the *or* in Igor meant gold.) But Diaghilev disliked the music so much that he cut the Terpsichore variation when the company was on tour, and would have done so in Paris, too, if I had not conducted all twelve performances there myself.

In *Apollo* I tried to discover a melodism free of folk-lore. The choice of another Classical subject was natural after *Oedipus Rex*, but Apollo and the Muses suggested to me not so much a plot as a signature, or what I already have called a manner. The Muses do not instruct Apollo—as a god he is already a master beyond instruction—but show him their arts for his approval.

The real subject of *Apollo*, however, is versification, which implies something arbitrary and artificial to most people, though to me art is arbitrary and must be artificial. The basic rhythmic patterns are iambic, and the individual dances may be thought of as variations of the reversible dotted-rhythm iamb idea. The length of the spondee is a variable, too, and so, of course, is the actual speed of the foot. The *pas d'action* is the only dance in which patterns of iambic stress are not immediately apparent, but the subtlety of that piece, if I may say so, is in the way the iamb is saved for the subsidiary key and then developed in augmentation at the return of the original key. I cannot say whether the idea of the Alexandrines, that supremely arbitrary set of prosodic rules, was pre-compositional or not—who can say where composition begins?—but the rhythm of the cello solo (at No. 41 in the Calliope variation) with the pizzicato accompaniment is a Russian Alexandrine suggested to me by a couplet from Pushkin, and it was one of my first musical ideas. The remainder of the Calliope variation is a musical exposition of the Boileau text that I took as my motto[7]. But even the violin cadenza is related to the versification idea. I thought of it as the initial solo speech, the first essay in verse of Apollo the god.

The success of *Apollo* as a ballet must be attributed to the dancing of Serge Lifar and to the beauty of Balanchine's choreography, especially to constructions such as the 'troika' in the Coda and the 'wheelbarrow' at the beginning, in which two girls support a third carrying Apollo's lute. But was it a success? The journalists, with characteristic perception, pointed out that it wasn't 'Greek,' and the English and Americans pretended to be disturbed by melodies which, they said, sounded like college songs (at No. 89—*The Boys from Syracuse*; at the fourth bar after No. 31; and at No. 22— 'shout to the rafters three'). The French were appalled at the suggestion of Delibes (at No. 68, for example) and Tchaikovsky (in Polyhymnia's variation, and at Nos. 34 and 69). And some people said that the beginning of the *pas de deux* had been stolen from

---

[7] *Que toujours dans vos vers, le sens coupant les mots,*
   Suspende l'hemistiche, en marque le repos. (*L'Art poétique.* I, 105 f.)
Pushkin criticized Boileau's 'pseudo-classicism', incidentally, saying that it 'never went further than the salon.'

Debussy's *Clair de lune*, and that the beginning of the whole work had been taken from the '*miserere*' of *Il Trovatore*.[8] The score was generally dismissed as light and even empty. I was hurt by this—as I considered it—misunderstanding. *Apollo* is a tribute to the French seventeenth century. I thought that Frenchmen might have taken the hint for this, if not from my musical Alexandrines, at least from the décors: the chariot, the three horses, and the sun disc (the Coda) were the emblem of *le roi soleil*.[9] But if a truly tragic note is sounded anywhere in my music, that note is in *Apollo*. Apollo's birth is tragic, I think, and so is his ascent to Parnassus, and the Apotheosis is every bit as tragic as Phèdre's line when she learns of the love of Hippolyte and Aricie—'*Tous les jours se levaient clairs et sereins pour eux*'—though, of course, Racine and myself were both absolutely heartless people, and cold, cold.

Apollo was my largest single step toward a long-line polyphonic style, and though it has a harmonic and melodic, above all an intervallic, character of its own, it nourished many later works as well. For example, the last seven measures of Apollo's first variation might equally have come from *Orpheus*, and the section at No. 212 in Act II of *The Rake* is purely Apollonian, and I do not mean the 'philosophy,' but the notes. (Bits of old pieces are always turning up in new ones, and two other examples have just occurred to me: the string theme in the *Scherzo fantastique* is recalled in the *Firebird* by the trumpets two measures before No. 14; and, though composed almost forty years apart, the cembalo octaves at No. 196 in Act III of *The Rake* have certainly come from the same wellsprings as the octaves in Death's music one measure after No. 123 in *The Nightingale*.) *Apollo* also was my first attempt to compose a large-scale work in which contrasts of volumes replace contrasts of instrumental colours. Volumes, incidentally, are all too rarely recognized as a primary musical element, and how few listeners have remarked the real joke in the *Pulcinella* duet, which is that the trombone has a very loud voice and the string bass has almost no voice at all.

[8] *Il Trovatore*, the 'Anvil Chorus,' is also supposed to be the source of the trombone march tune two measures before No. 187 in *Perséphone*, though I am certain I did not think of it just at the time, as I did not know the 'London Bridge is Falling Down' tune when I wrote the latter part of *Danses concertantes*.

[9] This chariot was attractively designed by Bauchant, and so was the curtain with bouquet *à la* Odilon Redon, but Bauchant's costumes had to be remade, by Chanel.

What do I love most in *Apollo*? The last six measures of Calliope; the coda of the Coda; the augmentation in the *pas d'action* and the cadence that leads from it to the violin solo; the false-relation cadence in the *pas d'action* (measures 4–5 of No. 29, and especially the viola E flat); the entire second variation of Apollo and the entire Apotheosis.

My *Aufführungspraxis* is concerned chiefly with rhythmic articulation, and if I had time to prepare a new edition now, I would mark every note to be played on or off the string, and give the bowing. The figure

from the beginning to No. 6 and from No. 15 to the end of the movement should be played as though double-dotted, and the thirty-second notes should be played as sixty-fourth notes. Double dotting, Budapest style, also applies to the violin solos in the second variation, in the cello solo at No. 59, the bass solo four measures before No. 63, and from No. 99 to the end of the movement. The notation of *fermati* is misleading two measures before No. 67, where the hold should apply only to the first cellos, and four measures before No. 23, where it is intended only for the solo violins. At No. 23 the violin cadenza should be played as a strict 3/8 measure grouped as follows:

seven even notes on the first eighth;

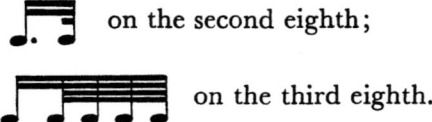

I would also like to warn cellists that the B-natural harmonic in the little homage-to-Saint-Saëns solo in Calliope lies very far back on the string, and is therefore usually played flat.

Here are a few additional points: 1. The appoggiaturas in the very first measure of the piece should be played almost as slowly as if they were the last two-thirds of a triplet. 2. At No. 4 the half-notes in violas, cellos, basses should be played as though the conductor were applying the sustaining pedal of a piano. 3. At three measures before 3, and again for the last two beats before 3, all parts require a small crescendo. 4. The time-scale seems to be too loose at two measures before 3 and at two measures before 6 but I feel this differently now than in 1928. 5. At 10 the appoggiaturas are on the beat (second violins), but at five before 12 they are before the beat. 6. At 17 the crescendo should continue through the downbeat of the third measure. 7. At 24 the appoggiaturas may be played as sixteenth notes. 8. At the second measure of 58 the appoggiaturas are before the beat. 9. The conductor should stay in two at 83; and obey the dynamics at 86, a passage that now sounds like something from *The Boy Friend*. 10. The tremolos in the Apotheosis are unmeasured, *i.e.*, faster than written.

Perséphone

R.C.: What do you recall of the original staging of *Perséphone* and what are your present ideas for staged presentations of the work?
I.S.: The unstaged preview performance at the Polignacs' is clearer in my recollection than the actual première, and I can still see the Princess's salon, myself groaning at the piano, Suvchinsky singing a loud and abrasive Eumolpus, Claudel glaring at me from the other side of the keyboard, Gide bridling more noticeably with each phrase.

The actual performance was visually unsatisfactory, which must be why my memory is so discreet about it, but the fact that I fail to remember the staging is surprising because the music was composed and timed to a fixed plan of stage action. The form is so specifically theatrical, in fact, that at least two episodes make little sense in concert performances: Pluto's mute march-aria for oboe and bass instruments, and the sarabande of the *raccourci* ending with the appearance of Mercury.

Perséphone is described in the score as a melodrama, a term C. S. Lewis defines as 'the tragic in exile.' It is, in fact, a masque or dance-pantomime co-ordinated with a sung and spoken text. Ida Rubinstein declaimed the text at the première, but she did not dance, which was as it should be, or so I now think. The mime should not speak, the speaker should not mime, and the part should be shared by two performers. I say this not only because few mimes, or dancers, are trained speakers as well (an argument refuted by Vera Zorina, who is skilled both as a dancer and *diseuse*, and who is beautiful to look at as well—what a superorbital ridge!), but also, and principally, because the division of labour allows greater freedom for mimetic movement. This is important if only for the reason that Perséphone's longest soliloquies are musically motionless, but also because I now think it stylistically wrong to grant one stage figure unique powers of speech: the sound of Perséphone's voice always comes as a shock, after a wordless section of mimed or danced movements.

The speaker Perséphone should stand at a fixed point antipodal to Eumolpus, and an illusion of motion should be established between them. The chorus should stand apart from and remain outside the action. The resulting separation of text and movement would mean that the staging could be worked out entirely in choreographic terms. (Balanchine would have been the ideal choreographer, Tchelitchev the ideal decorator.) At the première, Eumolpus stood deep downstage on a tall pedestal, just out of sight of my beat and just out of hearing. The chorus did not move, though this was not in accord with any aesthetic plan, but only because their labour union wouldn't let them. Pluto and Mercury did not appear in the original production, but they should appear, I think, and Tryptolemus and Demeter as well, if only because any embodiment will help to dramatize Gide's undramatic narrative. Demeter must be related both by costume and stage position to Eumolpus, who is her priest. But narcissuses and pomegranates are better kept in the cupboard of comic props now associated with the Gide-Wilde age.

My first recommendation for a *Perséphone* revival would be to commission Auden to fit the music with new words, as Werfel did *La Forza del Destino*. The rhymes are leaden-eared:

> *Perséphone confuse*
> *Se refuse*.

(I composed the music for this couplet on a train near Marseilles whose rhythm was anapaestic.) And the text borders, at times, on unconscious comedy; '*ivre de nuit . . . encore mal reveillée*,' for example, sounds like the description of a hangover. Gide was an anti-poet, as I think his poetry anthology shows.

But whether *Perséphone* is the patchwork and the bonbon that its critics claim is not for me to say, nor will time tell any more than a circumstantial truth. As for the critics, I must remark that no one has cited as stylistically discordant the section that I grafted whole from a sketch book of 1917 (the G minor flute and harp music in Eumolpus' second aria in Part II). But then, neither has anyone noticed that the two clarinets in the middle section of the Sarabande anticipate boogie-woogie by a decade.

Perséphone begins tentatively, the B flat music in 3/8 metre near the end is long, and the melodramas beget large stretches of *ostinato*. I am no longer able to evaluate such things, or ever again be as I was when I wrote *Perséphone*. But I still love the music, especially the flutes in Perséphone's final speech (this needs stage movement!), and the final chorus (when it is played and sung in tempo, and quietly, without a general *crescendo*). I love the chord before the C minor Russian Easter music, and I love the lullaby, '*Sur ce lit elle repose.*' I composed this *berceuse* for Vera de Bosset in Paris during a heat wave, and I wrote it originally to my own Russian words.

PROGRAMME NOTES

Octuor

R.C.: Would you describe the circumstances attending the composition of the *Octuor*?

I.S.: The *Octuor* began with a dream in which I saw myself in a small room surrounded by a small group of instrumentalists playing some very attractive music. I did not recognize the music, though I strained to hear it, and I could not recall any feature of it the next day, but I do remember my curiosity—in the dream—to know how many the musicians were.[1] I remember too that after I had counted them to the number eight, I looked again and saw that they were playing bassoons, trombones, trumpets, a flute, and a clarinet. I awoke from this little concert in a state of great delight and anticipation and the next morning began to compose the *Octuor*, which I had had no thought of the day before, though for some time I had wanted to write an ensemble piece—not incidental music like the *Histoire du soldat*, but an instrumental sonata.

The *Octuor* was quickly composed (in 1922). The first movement came first and was followed immediately by the waltz in the second movement. I derived the *tema* of the second movement from the waltz, which is to say that only after I had written the waltz did I discover it as a subject for variations. I then wrote the 'ribbons of scales' variation as a prelude to each of the other variations.

The final, culminating variation, the *fugato*, is my favourite episode in the *Octuor*. The plan of it was to present the theme in

[1] This confession exposes me to Minkowski's analysis of the counting mania as a time frustration, *i.e.*, of the compulsion to count as a wish to force future time, while the succubi at one's back push one into a false imagination. But time-dreams and counting-dreams are common with me, and so are dreams in which people shout, but inaudibly, like a cinema when the sound track fails, or talk out of hearing in the distance. I dream regularly now, too, that I am able to walk without a cane, as I could five years ago.

rotation by the instrumental pairs—flute-clarinet, bassoons, trumpets, trombones—which is the idea of instrumental combination at the root of the *Octuor* and of my dream. The third movement grew out of the *fugato*, and was intended as a contrast to that high point of harmonic tension. Bach's two-part Inventions were somewhere in the back of my mind while composing this movement, as they were during the composition of the last movement of the Piano Sonata. The terseness and lucidity of the inventions were an ideal of mine at that time, in any case, and I sought to keep those qualities uppermost in my own composition. What could be more terse than the punctuation of the final chord, in which the first inversion suffices to indicate *finis* and at the same time gives more flavour than the flat-footed tonic?

My appetite was whetted by my rediscovery of sonata form and by my pleasure in working with new instrumental combinations. I like the instrumental games in the *Octuor* and I can add that I achieved in it exactly what I set out to do. (If I were to compile a textbook of instrumental usages, they would have to be chosen from my own works only, for the reason that I could never be certain of the exact intentions of any other composer and therefore of the degree of his success or failure.)

I conducted the first performance in spite of a bad case of *trac*, owing to the occasion of it as the first concert work of mine which I introduced myself. The stage of the Paris Opéra seemed a large frame for only eight players, but the group was set off by screens, and the sound was well balanced. The *Octuor* was composed for and is dedicated to Vera de Bosset.

Four-hand Piano Music

R.C.: What attracted you to the medium of four-hand and two-piano music, and what were the circumstances of composition and performance in the case of the Eight Easy Pieces, the Sonata, and the Concerto?

I.S.: The Eight Easy Pieces were composed in Morges—the Polka, March, and Valse just before *Renard*, in 1915, the others after the completion of that burlesque. I wrote the Polka first, as a caricature of Diaghilev, whom I saw as a circus animal-trainer cracking a long whip. The idea of the four-hand duet was an aspect of the caricature also, because Diaghilev was very fond of four-hand piano playing which he had done with his lifelong friend Walter Nouvel[2] for as long as I had known him. The simplicities of one of the parts were designed in order not to embarrass the small range of Diaghilev's technique. I played the Polka to Diaghilev and Alfredo Casella in a hotel room in Milan in 1915, and I remember how amazed both men were that the composer of *Le Sacre du printemps* should have produced such a piece of popcorn. But for Casella a new path had been indicated, and he was not slow to follow it; so-called neoclassicism of a sort was born in that moment. But Casella was so genuinely enthusiastic about the Polka that I promised to write a little piece for him, too. This, the March, was composed immediately on my return to Morges. A little later I added the ice-cream wagon Valse in homage to Erik Satie, a souvenir of a visit to him in Paris. Satie, a very touching and attractive personality, suddenly had become old and white, though not less witty and gay. I tried to portray something of his *esprit* in the Valse. I orchestrated the Valse for seven solo instruments after composing it, and at the same time prepared a version of the Polka for cimbalom and small ensemble and of the March for eight solo players, but the March and Polka never have been published in this form. The other five pieces were composed as music lessons for my children Theodore and Mika. I wished to cultivate their love of music and to disguise my piano pedagogy by composing very easy parts for them to play, reserving the more difficult parts for the teacher, in this case myself, hoping thereby to give them a sense of performance participation. The Española was joined to the album after a trip to Spain, the Napolitana after a trip to Naples. Two of the Russian souvenirs, the Balalaika, which I like best of all of the eight pieces, and the Galop, were added at a later date, and the third, the Andante, like most preludes, was tacked on last. (Pascal: 'The last thing one discovers in composing a work is what to put first.') The Galop is a caricature of the St. Petersburg version of the Folies Bergères, which I had watched in the Tumpakov, a demi-respectable night club in the Astrava (the islands of the Neva on one of which my wife Vera was born). Ravel, hearing me conduct the Galop in the orchestral version, advised me to play it at a

[2] Nouvel had been a composer in his youth, one of the Petersburg *avant-garde* whose modernist tendencies irritated Rimsky-Korsakov. Another of Nouvel's piano partners was the poet Kusmin, whom I first met with Diaghilev at Nouvel's St. Petersburg home.

faster—the fastest possible—tempo, but I think that was because he mistook it for a cancan. The first concert performance of the Eight Easy Pieces was sponsored by Werner Reinhardt, in Lausanne. My co-pianist was the young José Iturbi.

I cannot discuss the Sonata and the Concerto now, for they require analysis and professional talk of a different kind, and what, dear programme annotator, can one *say* about a modulation or a plan of harmonic structure?

Both works were written for the love of 'pure art'—which is not only to say that they were not commissioned—and the geneses of the two were very different. The Sonata began as a piece for one performer, but was redesigned for two pianos when I saw that four hands were required to voice the four lines clearly.

I began the Sonata before and completed it after the *Scènes de ballet*. I have played it publicly only once, at a Mills College students' concert with Nadia Boulanger as my partner. I was staying with Darius Milhaud then, and the Sonata reminds me of an incident concerning the plumbing in the Milhaud house. One morning the lavatory drains stopped functioning. A plumber came, but we soon found that an archaeologist would have been more appropriate. Trenches had to be dug; the Milhauds had been emptying coffee grounds into the sink for years, and the pipe from their house to the street was silted solid with them.

The Concerto is symphonic in both volumes and proportions, and I think I could have composed it, especially the variation movement, as an orchestral work. But my purpose was otherwise. I needed a solo work for myself and my son, and I wished to incorporate the orchestra and do away with it. The Concerto was intended as a vehicle for concert tours in orchestra-less cities.

I began the composition in Voreppe and completed the first movement there immediately after finishing the Violin Concerto. I stopped composing then because I could not *hear* the second piano. All my life I have tried out my music as I have composed it, orchestral as well as any other kind, four hands at one keyboard. That way I am able to test it as I cannot when the other player is seated at another piano. When I took up the Concerto again, after finishing the *Duo Concertant* and *Perséphone*, I asked the Pleyel company to build me a double piano, in the form of a small box of two tightly-wedged triangles. I then completed the Concerto in my Pleyel studio, test-hearing it measure by measure with my son Soulima at the other keyboard.

The variations—originally the second movement—were separated from the *con moto* movement by three years and much change of musical focus. I started composing them as soon as *Perséphone* was completed, but I was interrupted again, this time, alas, by an appendectomy. My son Theodore had had a burst appendix and an emergency removal, and as the operation fascinated me, I decided to have my own appendix removed, however unlikely the danger of peritonitis in my own case. I forced the operation on my other children, also, and on Vera de Bosset and many of my friends—or, rather, to put myself in a better light, I recommended it highly. This surgical spree took place shortly after the première of *Perséphone* and just before I became a French citizen on June 10, 1934. I was still wobbly when I went to London at the end of that month to record *Les Noces*.

I had steeped myself in the variations of Beethoven and Brahms while composing the Concerto, and in Beethoven's fugues. I am very fond of my fugue, and especially of the after-fugue or fugue consequent, but, then, the Concerto is perhaps my 'favourite' among my purely instrumental pieces. The second movement, the *Notturno*, is not so much night music as after-dinner music, in fact, a digestive to the larger movements.

The first performance of the Concerto was sponsored by L'Université des Annales, a literary lecture society. I introduced the music with a fifteen-minute talk (which I would not like to see reprinted), and I read this little discourse before many of my later performances of the work, as well. The concert, in the Salle Gaveau, was a matinée, which we repeated the same evening for a different audience. I performed the Concerto many times with my son in Europe and in South America (Buenos Aires, Rosario), sometimes preceding it with the Mozart C minor fugue. After playing it in Baden-Baden in 1938, we made a commercial disc (for French Columbia) that was never released because of the War. I also performed the Concerto several times in the United States during the War, with the American pianist Adele Marcus. Once—in Worcester, Massachusetts, of all places—I introduced our performance of it with my old French lecture.

PROGRAMME NOTES

Symphony of Psalms

R.C.: Do you recall what determined your choice of texts in the Symphony of Psalms? What do you mean when you refer to the symbolism of the fugues? What was your first musical idea? Why did you employ a predominantly wind-instrument orchestra? What were the circumstances of the commission?

I.S.: The commissioning of the Symphony of Psalms began with the publisher's routine suggestion that I write something popular. I took the word, not in the publisher's meaning of 'adapting to the understanding of the people,' but in the sense of 'something universally admired,' and I even chose Psalm 150 in part for its popularity, though another and equally compelling reason was my eagerness to counter the many composers who had abused these magisterial verses as pegs for their own lyrico-sentimental 'feelings.' The Psalms are poems of exaltation, but also of anger and judgment, and even of curses. Although I regarded Psalm 150 as a song to be danced, as David danced before the Ark, I knew that I would have to treat it in an imperative way. My publisher had requested an orchestral piece without chorus, but I had had the psalm symphony idea in mind for some time, and that is what I insisted on composing. All of the music was written in Nice and in my summer home at Echarvines. I began with Psalm 150 and my first notation was the figure

that bears such a close resemblance to Jocasta's '*Oracula, oracula.*' After finishing the fast-tempo sections of the Psalm, I went back to compose the first and second movements. The Allelujah and the slow music at the beginning of Psalm 150, which is an answer to the question in Psalm 40, were written last.

I was much concerned, in setting the Psalm verses, with problems of tempo. To me, the relation of tempo and meaning is a primary question of musical order, and until I am certain that I have found the right tempo, I cannot compose. Superficially, the texts suggested a variety of speeds, but this variety was without shape. At first, and until I understood that God must not be praised in fast, *forte* music, no matter how often the text specifies 'loud,' I thought of the final hymn in a too-rapid pulsation. This is the manner question again. Can one say the same thing in several ways? *I* cannot, in any case, and to me the only possible way could not be more clearly indicated among all the choices if it were painted blue. I also cannot say whether a succession of choices results in a 'style,' but my own description of style is tact-in-action, and I prefer to talk about the action of a musical sentence than to talk about its style.

The first movement, 'Hear my prayer, O Lord,' was composed in a state of religious and musical ebullience. The sequences of two minor thirds joined by a major third, the root idea of the whole work, were derived from the trumpet–harp motive at the beginning of the *allegro* in Psalm 150. I was not aware of Phrygian modes, Gregorian chants, Byzantinisms, or anything of the sort, while composing this music, though influences said to be denoted by such scriptwriters' baggage-stickers may very well have been operative. Byzantium was a source of Russian culture, after all, and according to current indexing I am classified as a Russian, but the little I know about Byzantine music was learned from Wellesz long after I had composed the Symphony of Psalms. I did start to compose the Psalms in Slavonic, and only after coming a certain distance did I switch to Latin (just as I worked with English at the same time as Hebrew in *Abraham and Isaac*).

The 'Waiting for the Lord' Psalm makes the most overt use of musical symbolism in any of my music before *The Flood*. An upside-down pyramid of fugues, it begins with a purely instrumental fugue of limited compass and employs only solo instruments. The restriction to treble range was the novelty of this initial fugue, but the limitation to flutes and oboes proved its most difficult compositional problem. The subject was developed from the sequence of thirds used as an ostinato in the first movement. The next and higher stage of the upside-down pyramid is the human fugue, which does not begin without instrumental help for the reason that I modified the structure as I composed and decided to overlap instruments and voices to give the material more development; but the human choir is heard *a cappella* after that. The human fugue also represents a higher level in the architectural symbolism by the fact that it expands into the bass register. The third stage, the upside-down foundation, unites the two fugues.

PROGRAMME NOTES

Though I chose Psalm 150 first, and though my first musical idea was the already-quoted rhythmic figure in that movement, I could not compose the beginning of it until I had written the second movement. Psalm 40 is a prayer that a new canticle may be put into our mouths. The Allelujah is that canticle. (The word allelujah still reminds me of the Hebrew galosh-merchant Gurian who lived in the apartment below ours in St. Petersburg, and who on High Holy Days would erect a prayer tent in his living-room and dress himself in an ephod. The hammering sounds as he built this tent and the idea of a cosmopolitan merchant in a St. Petersburg apartment simulating the prayers of his forefathers in the desert impressed my imagination as profoundly as any direct religious experience of my own.) The rest of the slow-tempo introduction, the *Laudate Dominum*, was originally composed to the words of the *Gospodi Pomiluy*. This section is a prayer to the Russian image of the infant Christ with orb and sceptre. I decided to end the work with this music also, as an apotheosis of the sort that had become a pattern in my music since the epithalamium at the end of *Les Noces*. The *allegro* in Psalm 150 was inspired by a vision of Elijah's chariot climbing the Heavens; never before had I written anything quite so literal as the triplets for horns and piano to suggest the horses and chariot. The final hymn of praise must be thought of as issuing from the skies, and agitation is followed by 'the calm of praise'—but such statements embarrass me. What I can say is that in setting the words of this final hymn, I cared above all for the *sounds* of the syllables, and I have indulged my besetting pleasure of regulating prosody in my own way. I really do tire of people pointing out that *Dominum* is one word and that its meaning is obscured the way I respirate it, like the Allelujah in the *Sermon*, which has reminded everybody of the *Psalms*. Do such people know nothing about word-splitting in early polyphonic music? One hopes to worship God with a little art if one has any, and if one hasn't, and cannot recognize it in others, then one can at least burn a little incense.

My first sound-image was of an all-male chorus and *orchestre d'harmonie*. I thought, for a moment, of the organ, but I dislike the organ's *legato sostenuto* and its blur of octaves, as well as the fact that the monster never breathes. The breathing of wind instruments is one of their primary attractions for me. I obtained a satisfactory all-male chorus only once, to my recollection, and that was in Barcelona with the *Orfeo Català*, whose two hundred little boys, with their mamas and relatives, almost filled the hall. I was careful to keep the treble parts within the powers of child choristers.

Violin Concerto

R.C.: Would you say something about your Violin Concerto, the background, the genre, the later career of the piece as a ballet?

I.S.: The Concerto was commissioned for Samuel Dushkin by his patron, the American gentleman Blair Fairchild. Fairchild had discovered Dushkin and his talent for the violin at an early age, and had sponsored his education and career thereafter. The publisher Willy Strecker also helped in persuading me to accept the commission, and Strecker was a friend of Dushkin, too. Dushkin conferred with me often during the composition, and thus began a friendship that is now more than thirty years old.

The first two movements of the Concerto and part of the third movement were composed in Nice, but the score was completed at La Vironnière, a château near Voreppe which I rented from a country lawyer who looked like Flaubert. I was very fond of this house, and especially of my attic workroom, which had a fine view of the Val d'Isère, but the inconveniences of country life and the need to drive to Grenoble for provisions were too much for me and I eventually had to move.

The Violin Concerto was not inspired by or modelled on any example. I did not find that the standard violin concertos—Mozart's, Beethoven's, or even Brahms's—were among their composers' best work. (The Schoenberg concerto is an exception, but that is hardly standard yet.) The subtitles of my Concerto—Toccata, Aria, Capriccio—may suggest Bach, and so, in a superficial way, might the musical substance. I am very fond of the Bach Concerto for Two Violins, as the duet of the soloist with a violin from the orchestra in the last movement of my own Concerto may show. But my Concerto employs other duet combinations too, and the texture is almost always more characteristic of chamber music than of orchestral music. I did not compose a cadenza, not because I did not care about exploiting the violin virtuosity, but because the violin in combination was my real interest. But virtuosity for its own sake has only a small role in my

Concerto, and the technical demands of the piece are relatively tame.

Balustrade (1940), the ballet that George Balanchine and Pavel Tchelitchev made of the Violin Concerto, was one of the most satisfactory visualizations of any of my works. Balanchine composed the choreography as he listened to my recording, and I could actually observe him conceiving gesture, movement, combination, composition. The result was a series of dialogues complementary to and co-ordinated with the dialogues of the music.[3] The *corps de ballet* was small, and the second Aria was a solo piece for Tamara Toumanova. *Balustrade* was produced by Sol Hurok, that savant of the box office, and it must have been his first and last misjudgment in that sense. The set exposed a white balustrade on a dark stage, and the costumes were sinuous patterns in black and white.

I first knew the late Pavel Tchelitchev in Berlin in 1922, during the time I spent there waiting to meet my mother, who was leaving Russia. I considered him more gifted as a theatrical designer than as an easel painter, but that is probably because he decorated my own ballets—*Apollo* as well as *Balustrade*—so extremely well. I was especially fond of his costumes for Giraudoux's *Ondine*, also, and I had a good opportunity to watch him work then, as they were executed for him by my niece Ira Belline. Tchelitchev had a queer and difficult character, for though lively and very attractive as a person, he was also morbidly superstitious, and he would wear a mysterious red thread around his wrist or talk hieratically about the Golden Section and the true meaning of Horapollo.

Scènes de Ballet

R.C.: Did you have a narrative or choreographic scheme in mind composing the *Scènes de Ballet*, and did the fact of the commission for a Broadway extravaganza influence the musical substance and style? What is your present view of this music?

I.S.: When Billy Rose telephoned me one spring day in 1944 with an offer of five thousand dollars for a fifteen-minute ballet suite, he said that my solo dancers would be Alicia Markova and Anton Dolin and that Dolin would compose the choreography. But in

---

[3] Hofmannsthal to Strauss: 'Ballet is perhaps the only form of art which permits real, intimate collaboration between two people gifted with visual imagination.'

spite of Dolin, the choreography was my own, in the sense that I conceived the sequence, character, and proportions of the pieces myself and visualized the dance construction of this plotless, 'abstract' ballet as I wrote the music. In fact, no other score of mine prescribes a choreographic plan so closely.

The orchestral introduction exposes two identifying devices, the blues chord, and the melodic-pull idea:

When the curtain opens (at No. 5) the *corps de ballet* is discovered dancing in groups. The melodic-pull music is played by four violas and danced by four ballerinas. At No. 9 the groups join together, and at No. 40 they exit as the ballerina enters, *sola*. The idea of the Pantomime was that different groups of dancers should enter from different positions, each group in co-ordination with one of the arpeggiated figures in the music. The *Andantino* is a solo dance for the ballerina. When I first played it to Markova and Dolin, in my house in Hollywood, they said the flute cascades suggested falling stars, but I am unaware whether any such pictorial nonsense was realized in the performance, or even whether this part of the piece was performed at all. My only scenic idea was that the ballerina should wear a black tutu with diamond sequins, her partner a classical gilet.

The music from Nos. 60 to 69 is a dance for the *corps de ballet*. The trumpet solo in the *pas de deux* is associated with the male dancer, the horn with the female. The frilled phrase-endings in the ballerina's *Allegretto* were conceived as possibilities for pirouettes. The recapitulation of the *pas de deux* with the full orchestra now sounds to me like—pardon the pleonasm—bad movie music: the happy homesteaders, having massacred the Indians, begin to plant their CORN. In the last two measures of this number the solo dancers disappear at opposite sides of the stage, and the second Pantomime is an ensemble for the *corps de ballet*. The orchestral *tutti* that follows is the male dancer's solo variation, and the cello duet is the ballerina's solo. The final Pantomime unites the solo dancers, and the rest of the score—from the jazz movement in 3/8 time to the Apotheosis—assembles the whole company. I envisaged, for the finale, a stage full of groups twirling and mounting '*delirando.*'

The story of the first performance of *Scènes de Ballet* (I did not know that Glazunov had used this title when I chose mine) is very worldly indeed. Page by page as I completed the orchestra score, my friend Ingolf Dahl arranged it for piano. Mr. Rose professed to like the music in this piano version, or so I was told, but he was dismayed by my orchestral cellophane. The music was cut to a fraction of its original length when *The Seven Lively Arts*, the show for which it was composed, opened in New York. After the first night of the Philadelphia preview run I received a telegram: YOUR MUSIC GREAT SUCCESS STOP COULD BE SENSATIONAL SUCCESS IF YOU WOULD AUTHORIZE ROBERT RUSSELL BENNETT RETOUCH ORCHESTRATION STOP BENNETT ORCHESTRATES EVEN THE WORKS OF COLE PORTER. I telegraphed back: SATISFIED WITH GREAT SUCCESS.

Scènes de Ballet is a period piece, a portrait of Broadway in the last years of the War. It is featherweight and sugared—my sweet tooth was not yet carious, then—but I will not deprecate it, not even the second Pantomime, and all of it is at least well made. I like the Apotheosis best of all and, especially, the voicing of the chords in the introduction to it, with the repetition of the upper line in canon and in different harmonic contexts. The Apotheosis was composed on the day of the liberation of Paris. I remember that I interrupted my work every few minutes to listen to the radio reports. I think my jubilation is in the music.

Symphony in Three Movements

R.C.: You have at times referred to your Symphony in Three Movements as a 'war symphony.' In what way is the music marked by the impression of world events?
I.S.: I can say little more than that it was written under the sign of them. It both does and does not 'express my feelings' about them, but I prefer to say only that, without participation of what I think of as my will, they excited my musical imagination. And the events that thus activated me were not general, or ideological, but specific: each episode in the Symphony is linked in my imagination

with a concrete impression, very often cinematographic in origin, of the war.

The third movement actually contains the genesis of a war plot, though I recognized it as such only after completing the composition. The beginning of that movement is partly, and in some—to me wholly inexplicable—way, a musical reaction to the newsreels and documentaries that I had seen of goose-stepping soldiers. The square march-beat, the brass-band instrumentation, the grotesque *crescendo* in the tuba—these are all related to those repellent pictures.

Though my visual impressions of world events were derived largely from films, they also were rooted in personal experience. One day in Munich, in 1932, I saw a squad of Brown Shirts enter the street below the balcony of my room in the Bayerische Hof and assault a group of civilians. The civilians tried to protect themselves behind sidewalk benches, but soon were crushed beneath these clumsy shields. The police arrived, eventually, but by then the attackers had dispersed. That same night I dined with Vera de Bosset and the photographer Eric Schall in a small Allee restaurant. Three men wearing swastika armbands entered the room, and one of them began to talk insultingly about Jews and to aim his remarks in our direction. With the afternoon street fight still in our eyes, we hurried to leave, but the now shouting Nazi and his myrmidons followed, cursing and threatening us the while. Schall protested, and at that they began to kick and hit him. Miss de Bosset ran to a corner, found a policeman, and told him that a man was being killed, but this piece of intelligence did not rouse him to any action. We were rescued by a timely taxi, and though Schall was battered and bloody, we went directly to a police court where the magistrate was as little perturbed with our story as the policeman had been. 'In Germany today, such things happen every minute,' was all he said.

To return to the plot of the movement, in spite of contrasting episodes, such as the canon for bassoons, the march music is predominant until the fugue, which is the stasis and the turning point. The immobility at the beginning of the fugue is comic, I think— and so, to me, was the overturned arrogance of the Germans when their machine failed. The exposition of the fugue and the end of the Symphony are associated in my plot with the rise of the Allies, and perhaps the final, albeit rather too commercial, D flat sixth chord—instead of the expected C—tokens my extra exuberance in the Allied triumph. The figure

$$\eighth\quad \eighth\quad \eighth\eighth$$

was developed from the rumba in the timpani part in the introduction to the first movement. It was associated in my imagination with the movements of war machines.

The first movement was likewise inspired by a war film, this time a documentary of scorched-earth tactics in China. The middle part of the movement—the music for clarinet, piano, and strings, which mounts in intensity and volume until the explosion of the three chords at No. 69—was conceived as a series of instrumental conversations to accompany a cinematographic scene showing the Chinese people scratching and digging in their fields.

The formal substance of the Symphony—perhaps Three Symphonic Movements would be a more exact title—exploits the idea of counterplay among several types of contrasting elements. One such contrast, the most obvious, is that of harp and piano, the principal instrumental protagonists. Each has a large *obbligato* role and a whole movement to itself and only at the turning-point fugue, the *queue de poisson* of the Nazi machine, are the two heard together and alone.

But enough of this. In spite of what I have said, the Symphony is not programmatic. Composers combine notes. That is all. How and in what form the things of this world are impressed upon their music is not for them to say.

Jazz Commercials

R.C.: What were the origins of your pieces for so-called jazz and other popular band ensembles—the *Circus Polka, Scherzo à la russe, Ebony Concerto, Ragtime* for eleven instruments—and how do you regard this music today?
I.S.: With the exception of the *Ragtime*, these were all journeyman jobs, commissions I was forced to accept because the war in Europe had so drastically reduced the income from my compositions. The idea of the *Circus Polka* was George Balanchine's. He wanted a short piece for a ballet of elephants, one of whom was to carry Vera Zorina, who was at that time Balanchine's wife. The

Marche militaire quotation came to me as an absolutely natural thing, which I say to circumvent the inevitable German professor inevitably calling my use of it a parody. The music was first performed in someone else's arrangement by the Ringling Brothers' Circus Band. After conducting my orchestral original, in Boston in 1944, I received a congratulatory telegram from Bessie, the young pachyderm who had carried the *bella ballerina* and who had heard my broadcast in the winter quarters of the circus at Sarasota. I never saw the ballet, but I met Bessie in Los Angeles once and shook her foot.

The *Scherzo à la russe* was commissioned by Paul Whiteman for a special radio broadcast. I wrote it originally to exact specifications of his ensemble, then rewrote it for standard orchestra—which gave me some trouble, as the volume of mandolin and guitar in the Trio canon was so much lighter than that of harp and piano. Whiteman conducted the first performance himself, much too rapidly. He and others professed to hear reminiscences of *Petrushka* in it.

The *Ebony Concerto* was also written for a prescribed instrumentation, to which I added a French horn. Mr Woody Herman wanted the piece for a concert that already was scheduled, and I had to compose it in a hurry. My plan was to write a jazz *concerto grosso* with a blues slow movement. I studied recordings of the Herman band and enlisted a saxophonist to teach me to finger. 'Ebony' does not mean 'clarinet', incidentally, but 'African.' The only jazz I had heard in the United States was in Harlem, and by Negro bands in Chicago and New Orleans, and the jazz performers I most admired at that time were Art Tatum, Charlie Parker, and the guitarist Charles Christian. And blues meant African culture to me.

I conducted, not the première performance, but the recording in Los Angeles some weeks later. What I remember most clearly was the smoke in the recording studio. When the musicians did not blow horns they blew smoke, and of such tangibility that the atmosphere looked like Pernod clouded by water. Their instrumental mastery was astonishing, but so was their lack of *solfeggio*. Of the four pieces you name I like the *Ebony Concerto* best, though it is remote from me now, like the work of a sympathetic colleague I once knew well.

Jazz—blanket term—has exerted a time-to-time influence on

my music since 1918, and traces of blues and boogie-woogie can be found even in my most 'serious' pieces, as, for example, in the *Bransle de Poitou* and the *Bransle simple* from *Agon* and in the *pas d'action* and *pas de deux* (middle section) from *Orpheus*. In 1918 Ernest Ansermet, returning from an American tour, brought me a bundle of ragtime music in the form of piano reductions and instrumental parts, which I copied out in score. With these pieces before me, I composed the *Ragtime* in *Histoire du soldat*, and, after completing *Histoire*, the *Ragtime* for eleven instruments. The *Histoire* ragtime is a concert portrait, or snapshot of the genre—in the sense that Chopin's *Valses* are not dance waltzes, but portraits of waltzes. The snapshot has faded, I fear, and it must always have seemed to Americans like very alien corn. If my subsequent essays in jazz portraiture were more successful, that is because they showed awareness of the idea of improvisation, for by 1919 I had heard live bands and discovered that jazz performance is more interesting than jazz composition. I am referring to my non-metrical pieces for piano solo and clarinet solo, which are not real improvisations, of course, but written-out portraits of improvisation.

I began the *Ragtime* for eleven instruments in October 1918 and finished it on the morning of the Armistice. I remember how, sitting at the cimbalom in my garret in Morges, like *Gretchen am Spinnrade*, I was aware of a buzzing in my ears that increased until I was afraid I had been stricken like Robert Schumann. I went down to the street and was told that everyone was hearing the same noise and that it was from cannon along the French frontier announcing the end of the war.

I composed the *Ragtime* on the cimbalom, and the whole ensemble is grouped around the bordello-piano sonority of that instrument. I continued to play the cimbalom every day in my Pleyel[4] Studio in Paris between the wars, though I wrote no more music for it because of the difficulty of finding good players. Nevertheless, some of the piano writing in my *Capriccio* is cimbalomist in style, especially the cadenza in the second movement, which is a kind of Rumanian restaurant music.

When the composition was completed, I asked Picasso to design a cover. I watched him draw six figures, each from a single, uninterrupted line. He chose the published one himself.

[4] The Pleyel company constructed new pedals that I designed for the instrument, and they tuned it regularly.

With Ernest Ansermet and Prokofiev, Talloires, 1929.

With Ramuz, 1932.

My father's grave in Leningrad, photographed in 1925.

INTERVIEWS

The Musical Scene and Other Matters

'*Where is any certain tune or measured music in notes such as these?*'
Elizabeth Barrett Browning

New York Review of Books: Did you fly in from California, Mr. Stravinsky? How was it?
I.S.: If you mean Los Angeles, as sunless as a mushroom farm; if the flight, well, at least the muzak is no longer compulsory (speaking as one who prefers the aching void). But I will not complain about aeroplanes. I am unable to walk around the block any more, yet I can zoom around the world. There was some 'turbulence,' though, which interfered with the in-flight movie (a comedy that was no laughing matter) and the pilot made an announcement that has stuck in my mind ever since. He said that the IBM flight plan for the day had chosen 33,000 feet as the favoured altitude, but in his opinion we should be higher. This unexpected and touchingly obsolete criticism of computer authority shocked me, I confess, and I sincerely hope that the relationships of men and their computerology (and, conversely, the computerology of men and their relationships) become more trusting in time. Part of my shock may also have come from the contrast inherent in the fact of a computerized flight control and my memories of the Homeric air age of Saint-Exupéry, who was guided at times by little more than his own apprehensions. But the principal part was due to the circumstance that in my own work I regard my feelings as more reliable than my calculations.
N.Y.R.: Would you explain the distinction, Mr. Stravinsky?
I.S.: It was an empty one, I suppose; and in any case it is as impossible to draw sharp lines between verbal concepts of this sort as it is to draw them between analytical and empirical truths, or

between learned and innate behaviour. Our calculations and our feelings overlap and they may even be congruent. I will persist, nevertheless, and say that I trust my musical glands above the foolproofing of my musical flight charts, though I realize that the flight charts are formed in part by these same glands; and add that I think the tendency which seeks to attribute every factor in a musical composition to a punch-card master plan could constrict the 'free' options of the ear. If, however, I assert that the present supreme authority of mathematics in the arts is the result of a deep-rooted modern superstition, that is mere *ipse dixit* talk: it says something only about myself. And, please forgive me, now, at my age that is the kind of talk I prefer. For one thing, I do not have to use so many escape words, and for another, the subject—myself—is closer to home.

N.Y.R.: You have criticized option-of-the-moment arguments in the past, Mr. Stravinsky. Are you hinting at a reopening of the doors?

I.S.: I have criticized them not in composition but in performance—though that will be an unacceptable distinction to the happening school—and on performance my views have hardened rather than changed. Let me say that to me a happening is a composition, at least in retrospect. Soon someone will discover that it can be more interesting by being one before and during its performance as well, with which the cycle can begin all over again with Bach or Tubal Cain. Already the German orchestras refuse to participate in happenings or perform unwritten or incompletely notated music, which, however, I take not as a portent of the next step but as the simple reaction of good soldiers in need of explicit orders. Then what, we may ask, does 'next' mean? Even while I have been talking the 'next' will have become the 'former.' Conformism is so hot on the heels of the mass-produced *avant-gardes* that the 'ins' and the 'outs' change places with the speed of Mach III. Gone are the days when an art movement seemed to exist together with a political one (then falling with it as, for example, total serialization disappeared with deStalinization, and *musique concrète* with the unpersoning of Khrushchev). Who can say, any more, at any exact moment, whether it is Nono who is holding up sinking Venice or the other way around?

N.Y.R.: What is your view of the present state of traditional performance, Mr. Stravinsky, and how do you think the increased quantity of our music and the greater competition affect qualitative standards?

I.S.: Before I attempt to say anything about that let me offer a comment fresh from my own experience. We all know, or should know, that America produces the finest instrumentalists in the world, though the reasons are mysterious, orchestra players being as ill paid on the whole as poets or school teachers. This knowledge did not prepare me for the abundance of performing talent of the highest quality that I have discovered of late on visits to colleges and music schools such as Oberlin, Eastman, the University of Texas. And that said, I must add that I found not only talent but a sensible new generation of human beings. Last spring at an agricultural college in Indiana I saw my *Oedipus Rex* in an excellent production by students whose other time, for all I know, was occupied with lectures on fertilizer. Then, only a few weeks ago I heard the Eastman School orchestra play to perfection, on a minimum of rehearsal, some of my most difficult later music, including parts of *The Flood*, which at least one renowned professional orchestra could not manage after a week of rehearsals and a dozen performances. The flexibility of the young versus the rigidity of the *routiniers* is an old theme, of course, but you can hardly imagine the pleasure this student orchestra gave me.

To your question about quantity, quality, the effects of competition, I suggest that the classic criticisms of these capitalist concepts by Veblen and others may also be applied to music. The prior questions are the same, at any rate. Competition to what end? What standards, and in what ways are they improved? I have just heard a conductor improve a work of mine with beauty treatments, *i.e.*, daubing the music with lipstick and smothering it with face powder. Such things are both a form and result of competition, but of conductors' competition about conducting, or call it the performance of performance: they are in no wise a musical matter. The performance of performance has developed to such an extent in recent years that it challenges the music itself and will soon threaten it with relegation. I have seen performances (of performance) as fully worked out as a sonata, as neatly contrived as a fugue. The new conductor, X, for example, controls every stage of the operation as thoroughly as a cradle-to-grave social welfare plan, from a first entrance that exudes just the right amount of artistic mystique to a final few dozen exhausted bows.

I will not attempt to describe the performance that X employs with the actual music except to say that its most winning features are a crucifixion, the extended arms motionless and the hands limp in frozen passion; a pelvic thrust co-ordinated with a throwing back of the head, used at climaxes; and a turning of the profile not just toward the first violins but beyond them and out to the audience. Most of the other repertory is composed of stock mirror-the-music 'expression movements' (Lorenz's term for the same thing in geese ethology), but another innovation has been promised before the show reaches Broadway and according to rumour it will be handstands during inverted counterpoint. Still, the high point is none of these but the after-performance performance. It begins with a tableau modelled on the Descent from the Cross. The arms are lifeless, the knees are bent, the head (hair artfully disarrayed) is low, and the whole corpse is bathed in perspiration (warm water, one suspects, squirted from hidden atomizers). The first step down from the podium just fails to conceal a totter, but in spite of that the miracle-worker somehow manages to reappear forty-six times. It *is* a great performance, though, and could be topped as an advertisement only by skywriting. Even a musician could beswept away by it.

N.Y.R.: What new music have you heard recently, Mr. Stravinsky?
I.S.: New to me was the *Fanciulla del West*, a remarkably up-to-date TV horse opera with a Marshall Dillon and professional Indians like the lobby Indians in the hotels at Santa Fe. These aborigines are characterized, if you could call it that, by some ineffectual reminiscences of Debussy, but most of the score is back in the land of *Butterfly*; the opera is really an Eastern western. No matter what the geography, the music—self-parodying arias, a Roxy Theater overture—is bad. Why? Is it the absence of people with whom the composer could identify (they could not identify themselves, for sure)? Or the unsuitability of the subject to that genius of sentimentality which in *La Bohême* is so perfectly matched to the dramatic substance and so superbly deployed that even I leave the theatre, when I can get a ticket, humming my lost innocence? But there is one conspicuous success in *Fanciulla*, the attempt to make it American—*i.e.*, simple-minded—by having the gold miners sing in unison and by repeating a Grofé-type trot rhythm to the point of incandescence.

No doubt you mean newer music than that, but I am so out of

touch I can hardly tell a musical mobile from a musical stabile, let alone distinguish their splinter groups. What I hear, moreover, is what comes my way, and that is rarely of my own choosing. *Chronochromie*, by M. Malraux's favourite composer, came my way recently; its *force de frappe* is so great I wonder the marimbas, xylophones, and gongs did not collapse from metal fatigue. At about the same time I heard the same composer's *La Rousserolle effarvatte*, which proposes to do for the Reed Warbler (24 hours in the life of) something of what J. Joyce did for L. Bloom. (Well, I heard *some* of it.) I attended a programme of electronic music, too, but only one composition seemed to exist in and because of the medium, the others being translations, of which the best I can say is that they probably would have sounded still worse in their native tongues. The very thought of the paper work involved in producing these noises depresses me, for though I can sympathize with a Van Eyck labouring for months with a magnifying glass to paint a perfect beetle (and *not* for the reason that he didn't just blot or drip), I cannot understand musical composition that takes place outside of music. Better, now and then, one of those exhibitions of Anti-Music, though I have also failed to keep touch with developments in that department if, indeed, there are any: the only sounds (at least) that reach me are the breast-beating and axe-grinding of the Anti-Musician claqueurs themselves. I have lately been exposed to an amount of the window-dressing kind of new music by Polish composers, also, and can report that the surface qualities of it are generally attractive—Tadeusz Baird's unprovoking (in the sense of the title) *Erotica*, for example—and that, well, feelings often seemed to have entered into calculations. More recently I have heard some striking scores by new French composers: Guézec's *Architectures colorées*, Eloy's *Equivalences*, Gilbert Amy's double-orchestra piece *Antiphonies*. There *is* a new French school, and a good one, judging by levels of skill. Boulez is its father figure, naturally, though he steers clear of the question of Dada.

One of the two most impressive recent musical experiences—the other was *Jacob's Ladder*—I owe to the late Noah Greenberg and the tapes of polyphonic singing recorded by him in mountain villages near Tiflis. Greenberg's discovery of an active performing tradition of music ranging from tenth-century conductus and organum to High Renaissance was a major find, I think, contributions to performance knowledge being even more valuable than acquisitions of more music—and this time the line *can* be drawn. The yodelling, called Krimanchuli in Georgian, used in the performance of *trecento* hockets, is the most virile vocal performance I have ever heard. Needless to say, this exhumed treasure, being both foreign and religious in origin and therefore embarrassing to progressive historicism, and polyphonic and therefore subversive, is unwelcome in the Soviet Union and unlikely to be preserved. No doubt it will be ploughed under again for good, and replaced by Moscow-manufactured party-slogan songs. The decline of culture in musical terms—if you will excuse a bit of my own historicism—is the devolution from polyphony to monophony.

Jacob's Ladder is described as a 'sketch' and a 'torso,' and both descriptions are correct but misleading. The notes are Schoenberg's but not the colour, though enough of that, too, is the composer's own to direct and imprint the mixtures by another hand. Admittedly, where the instrumentation was completed by Schoenberg, as in the latter part of the music of *One Dying*, the difference is devastating; and where the composer's instrumental indications are sparse, as in the music of *One Wrestling*, the realization is hopelessly conventional and the rate of change in orchestral combinations obviously too slow. There are also, I think, some wrong interpretations, as in the accompaniment to the word '*Rhythmus*' at the end of the music of *One of the Called*, where the voice-leading indicates that the same timbre could not have been intended for both the top line at the beginning of the measure and the third line at the end of it. Still, in spite of the orchestration and the incompleteness, the existing segment is one of the highest achievements of our music.

The use of multiple orchestras and speaking choruses is responsible for much special-pleading Schoenberg-Crusade talk about the prophetic nature of the score, but the reincorporation of tonality which the composer himself had excommunicated eight years earlier is as remarkable. The use of it with the words of *The Indifferent* and *The Resigned* is pointed, of course, but it is integrated in other places as well and throughout the score, while octave doublings occur regularly, and in parallel form as in the introduction to Gabriel's speech 'This Either or this Or.' Whether in consequence of these 'levities' or not, the harmony is the richest Schoenberg ever wrote. The *Glückliche Hand*, together with the *Four Orchestral Songs*, supplies a rudimentary context for the opening, but Schoenberg does not tarry at past points of connection and the music unfolds

in continuous upward progression until, on the threshold of a new world of sound, the manuscript comes to an end. Here Franz Joseph gained a conscript.
N.Y.R.: You said it was easier for you to talk about yourself, Mr. Stravinsky. May I ask what it is like to be eighty-four?
I.S.: There is no triumph in it, I can tell you, and hardly any exhilaration. I am forgetful, repetitive, and deaf, for which reasons I tend to avoid all but Russian language conversations and in consequence to read more than ever before. Therefore when I talk, I talk too much, as you see, which is an irony, because I do not believe in words, not, at least, as I believe in music, and would erase all of my own if I had the power. A still more serious complaint than these, to me, is the diminishing of my working day, for though my composing speed is unslackened, the time allotted to it, due to the slower tempo of my other activities and to the greater demands on my time from lawyers, merchants, and especially doctors, evaporates more quickly. As a sufferer from polycythemia I am obliged to have a blood test every seventh day of my life and bleedings every two months—shades of the eighteenth-century barbershop—the containment of the disease by radio-active phosphorus no longer being safe in my case. (I used to swallow capsules of this alarming substance in a glass of fizz fed to me with lead-tipped calipers by a technician in an asbestos suit and a mask like a bee-keeper.) The cycle of the thickening and thinning of my blood has imposed a rhythm not only on my temperament (I go from concessive to obdurate), but on my whole creative life.

I suffer, too, as rarely before and as I have never admitted, from my musical isolation, as well as from a feeling of loneliness—this for the first time in my life—for my generation: all of my contemporaries are dead. It is not so much old friends or individuals that I regret, and certainly not the mentality of my generation, but the background as a whole, the habits of the home, the social intercourse, or call it the body. I am obliged to live now at a detached and strictly mind-level of exchange with younger people who represent, as they say, wholly different belief systems and who see me as an elderly crackpot always in a snit. This homesickness is very recent, though, and until a decade ago I forbade all mention of Russia and fled every reminder of my past.
N.Y.R.: What do you mean by your musical isolation, Mr. Stravinsky? No serious composer has exercised greater influence,

received wider recognition, been more frequently performed in his lifetime than you have been. Is there no triumph in that? And have you never felt the sense not of isolation but of the very opposite, namely that you as much as anyone in the world are in powerful communication?

I.S.: Thank you, but I could hardly afford to see myself in that light; and the catalogue of my past works does not interest me as much as my actual work, which the catalogue tends to overshadow and for which, in any case, it has never earned me any credit cards. It may be satisfying to see loudly condemned new scores such as *Agon* and the *Movements* quietly taking their place among earlier regularly performed ones, but I do not think of it as a victory. And what I meant by isolation was at the professional level. While I hardly regret not belonging to a movement, and that the music I now produce answers no commercial and little other demand, I would like to exchange more than a few rapidly crossing glimpses with my colleagues. As it is now, I see eye to eye with no one.

N.Y.R.: Surely this is only the result of your own eminence, Mr. Stravinsky.

I.S.: A plague on eminence! I hardly dare cross the street any more without a convoy, and I am stared at wherever I go like an idiot member of a royal family or an animal in a zoo; and zoo animals have been known to die from stares. 'This is probably the last time we will see *him*,' the eyes all seem to say, though I dare say a few of those onlookers may still pass on a bit ahead. No doubt there is a limbo of uncertainty concerning anyone who has been around as long as I have, and if middle-aged people are unsure, hearing my name, whether it belongs to a living person, young people automatically assume that a man of my *fin de siècle* connections *must* be dead.

N.Y.R.: What did you mean, a moment ago, when you declared your disbelief in words? Is it a question of their inexactness?

I.S.: They are not so much inexact as metaphorical; not so much another form of notation as an irrelevant and unedifying form. Sometimes I feel like those old men Gulliver encounters in the *Voyage to Laputa*, who have renounced language and who try to converse by means of objects themselves. A composer is always in that position: he has no verbal control over his music. Nowadays he tries to talk about it in graphs, statistical charts, symbolic codings, and other devices which may be more efficient—they are certainly more trenchant—than his statements in ordinary verbal syntax, but which bring him no nearer to the music. The one true comment on a piece of music is another piece of music.

N.Y.R.: May we ask what you are composing at present, Mr. Stravinsky?

I.S.: I can give you no more than labels; as I just said, I am unable to enter my work with words; the music says what it is and the music is self-contained. Until now—I have just completed the *Rex Tremendae*—I call it my pocket Requiem, both because I use only fragments of the text and interlard them with instrumental music (though there is precious little lard in it) and because most of it was composed in notebooks which I carry on my person. But I am superstitious and do not like to talk about any work in progress, let alone a monument ordered, like Mozart's, by a 'mysterious stranger.' I will be mightily relieved to be done with it and to get on to something else. At times during the composition I have derived comfort from the knowledge that my great-grandfather lived to the age of 111; and I have often wondered what he was like at 84. He did not compose music, to be sure, but—or so the family tradition goes—he was doing something very like it, which is making love. In fact, the old gentleman, bless his hormones, died as the result of a fall while trying to scale the garden fence on his way to a rendezvous. What a way to go, as the Americans say; and, better yet, what a time of life to go that way.

Music and the Statistical Age

Commentary: And how do you view the statistical life generally, Mr. Stravinsky?

I.S.: With misgivings, of course, but I have failed to arrive at anything so solid as a 'view,' being at best dimly, though not for that reason unprejudicially, aware of certain effects of the quantifications of society that have already taken place. But the quantifying of the entire mental world that is now in store and that supposes a new type of mind, or way of thinking, is a development I am powerless to imagine. Still, the incapacity for it has not prevented the question from invading my old-fashioned speculative mind a good deal of late.

C.: Why particularly 'of late'?

I.S.: It is difficult to say for certain. There are small encroachments of statistical philosophy all the time, but we notice them, concern ourselves with them, only when conscious that a whole new area has fallen. It was like that with automation. I had read about it inattentively during the last few years, then a month ago some first-hand experience jolted me like a judo throw. This occurred, surprisingly, in a tatty and down-at-heel Midwest hotel: I telephoned to order the *petit déjeuner* before going to bed and was answered by a recorded Mother Superior-type voice: 'This is your breakfast robot: after you hear the dial tone please give your name, room number, breakfast order, the time you wish it served. . . . beeep.' A silence followed, just long enough—it was sealed by another, terminal 'beeep'—to encompass a statistically averaged recitation of the requested facts from a properly organized customer. But I failed to remember the sequence of the questions, did not *know* my room number, neglected to say how to prepare the eggs, forgot to specify the time of service. Moreover, that final 'beeep' so exasperated me that when I did get organized I promptly recorded an order for two hundred pieces of burned toast to be sent to the three-hundredth floor at 4 a.m.: which is 'feedback' with a vengeance.

C.: But do you not believe that improved automation techniques controlled by the ever more sophisticated tools of statistical analysis can bring about a more efficient channelling of resources?

I.S.: I can say that recent errors in my bank statements have done little to promote confidence on at least *this* individual level. Nevertheless, in the great synthetic civilization of the totally automated future, we might reasonably expect a more equal distribution of certain kinds of wealth, and a consequent relief of so-called under-privileged peoples; and improvements in everyone's animal living habits, as the new science of ergonomics seems to promise (see the survey just published at Cornell on the mutual misfitting of the human anatomy and most bathroom appliances); and new techniques of conservation (not merely bloodbanks everywhere, but banks of frozen superior sperm as well, though to me this sounds depressingly like the whaling industry, in spite of the onesided amusement that the banking process may afford the eugenically selected depositors). Nor are some of the new kinds of mentalizing efficiency difficult to imagine, the propensities of the McLuhan-type literature of our own period being clear enough in such current best sellers as *The Cybernetics of Sexual Positions in*

INTERVIEWS

Relation to Socio-Economic Status, and *A Concordance of Views from the Perspex Penis*.

But I wonder about the other side, about the disadvantages, and about that new mind. Are we not equally justified in forecasting a mass conformism to statistics? After all, we know that more people than Francesca and Paolo have been seduced by books. We know, too, from an alarming nation-wide demonstration, that trend-analyses of vote tabulations in the Eastern United States are probably able to influence the vote in the Western time zones. Now, I am certainly *not* justified in inferring from these examples that conformisms to statistical findings are inevitable and irreversible; but I do infer it, nevertheless, because of my stealthy scepticism of most individual judgment and, correspondingly, my almost infinite faith in the powers of statistical persuasion, wish-imagining, suggestibility, mass attraction. I foresee the statistical philosophy becoming more and more circular, in fact, untidy figures being polished and rounded out; and, of course, trends being pushed to their conclusions; after all, to 'make the crooked straight' has been one of the most ruthlessly compulsive propositions in the history of our ethical geometries. When people are being informed by their statisticians that they might be developing cancer at a certain age—unless they have already died from the effects of strontium 90 at an earlier age—will they not, the poor lemmings, do their best to oblige?

And conformism is only one problem. What, for another, will become of the faculty of observation when exact prediction is a rule of life? Won't the observing mechanisms occupy a much smaller place in that new mind (on the analogy from physics according to which prediction by mathematical theory can precede observation, as in Yukawa's discovery of one of the meson-type particles)? This is mere prattle on my part, of course, for I know nothing about such matters myself, and still think sequentially, as the McLuhanites describe certain until recently respectable mental operations.

C.: Will you say something of the effects of quantification in music, Mr. Stravinsky?

I.S.: It will come to the same thing: on the one hand, greater efficiency in such important but peripheral matters as the computation of all sound elements, the discovery of a precise and economical notation, the formulation of a statistical theory of music equipped with a tangible terminology; and, on the other, a dangerous control at the heart of the matter, for McLuhan, if I understand him, is right. The new media are not merely new conveyors, but they are themselves conveyed: their forms and measurements will be stamped in the structure of that new mind. But here I am crystal-gazing again, and I have no gift for it. Unlike those shades in the Tenth Canto who see the past and the future but *not* the present, I see only the present. And besides, what I wished to suggest was that, for the moment at least, a backward look might be more instructive. Statistical philosophy in music seems to have been discovered some sixty years ago by Ives.

C.: Have you heard Ives' Fourth Symphony yet, Mr. Stravinsky, and if so, have you any comments to register concerning it?

I.S.: I have found it to be rather less of a 'gas' than opinion led me to expect. Ives was not primarily a symphonist; the *Three Places in New England* are more of an entity than any one of the symphonies (besides which they contain much better music than the third and more consistently good music than the fourth). But the second movement of the fourth is an astonishing achievement. The *in*clusiveness which is at the root of Ives' genius ('all things in their variety,' as he quoted Emerson) reaches saturation point in these seemingly free-for-all pages; 'seemingly' because while this or that tune may suddenly burst out for no other apparent reason than *joie de vivre*, it is inextricable in the skein of the composition. But I will say no more. I know too little of this fascinating composer who was exploring the 1960s during the heyday of Strauss and Debussy. Polytonality; atonality; tone clusters; tone rows; multiple orchestras; a rhythmic vocabulary which maintains a lead on the *avant-garde* even now; micro-intervals; perspectivistic effects; chance; statistical composition; permutation; add-a-part, practical-joke, and improvisatory music: these were Ives' discoveries a half-century ago as he quietly set about devouring the contemporary cake before the rest of us even found a seat at the same table. But to me personally these innovatory achievements are of less moment (artistic inventions not being patented, in any case) than my discovery in him, only very recently, of a new awareness of America.

C.: What was this discovery, Mr. Stravinsky? And since you have now lived almost as long here as in Russia, and longer here than in Western Europe, would you tell us some of your feelings about us?

Do you have a sense of identification with America, and what in America do you like most and dislike most?

I.S.: Identification, yes, but I cannot describe it or even be certain where and how it obtains. I can feel no identity with the present military version of the manifest destiny, and therefore no sympathy with the victims of peace-scares (*i.e.*, stock-market investors), but as I do not wish to provoke a visit from the C.I.A., I had better heed the advice of the Devil in my opera when he says, 'Let us not speak of that.' I do not identify very deeply with American music either, though I feel close to individual American musicians and to musical life in America. It seems to me that the greatest American art never tries to promote itself on the fact that it is homespun, yet Ives was ignored or written off as Americana precisely by the colonials of 'neo-classicism' and the '12-tone system,' and he seems to have survived only by crawling into that interesting New England woodwork.

But having said this much, I am at a loss to describe that personal discovery in Ives. My answer merely points in a general direction. Ives' music has told me more about what I think of as a peculiarly American feeling of isolation than the American outdoor novelists, Whitman or *Walden*, Miss Dickinson or Tuckerman (who felt 'the dark wind strain'). The qualities of it, like the dominant qualities of Ives, are alien to me, but they are an identifying link all the same, as I realize in Europe where differences of culture bring certain previously indistinguishable feelings into relief. In Europe, I often feel, against my heritage, that I belong to the American side; and I even confess to brief onsets of topographical nostalgia (more for Park Avenue and the reflections of clouds on tall glass buildings, I admit, than for those Midwestern parallelogram cities designed to be passed straight through), though I was never, in this regard, an exceptionally 'sticky' man. But to return to Ives, it seems to me time to consider the composer's share in his century along with the environmental factors of New England.

As for a compilation of likes and dislikes, that would constitute no more than a string of disembodied prejudices. I could say, for instance, that a salutation last year by the Mayor of Muncie (Indiana) touched me more than that of an eminent European Minister of Culture, because the degree of musical ignorance being equal in both, it seemed less excusable in the latter. Or, tipping the argument the other way, I could protest the American demolition mania, that neurotic need, now in peak phase, to repudiate the past. Some of the destruction—the impending demise of the Metropolitan Opera House, whose cornerstone postdated my own birth—strikes an old man as a personal offence. I had no very fond feelings for the Met, I confess, but now that it is empty I feel as if there had been a big death in New York, that a junior colleague of a kind has disappeared.

C.: And the *new* Metropolitan, Mr. Stravinsky, do you have any feelings about *that*? What do you foresee for *it*?

I.S.: Difficulties. It has lost most of its aura, a good deal of its alibi and practically all of its identity. But what *are* the reasons for centralizing a city's art commodities?—excuse the expression, but supermarkets for the arts, art shopping centres, is what they seem to be. Does no one fear that, lumped together, the characters of the individual institutions will tend to blur? Is environmental diversity a discredited idea?

C.: Do you feel the same way about the Kennedy Arts Center, Mr. Stravinsky?

I.S.: I have no feelings about it yet, but the latter two-thirds of the title hardly fall pit-a-pat on my ear. I foresee huge buildings—the more marginal the contents of the art the larger and more stolid the containers—tumbled about like blocks in low-scoring Stanford-Binet tests. The largest of them I picture as the 'Research Laboratory for the Readjustment of Acoustics in New Concert Halls'; and the second largest, the 'Hall of Fame for Heroes of Public Relations'—impresarios, orchestra conductors, patronesses, and others who have won or purchased a brief moment in the annals of publicity, here paid off with monuments in appropriately 'soft sculpture' (doomed to instant dissolution if the air conditioning should fail). It is disagreeable to say, but the art centres emphasize performance and exhibition at the expense of making and creating. That, however, and for a wonder, is the last sour note, toned down as it is, that I intend to blow today and, though I cannot guarantee not to backslide, I hope that it will be my farewell appearance this season as a 'heavy.' For a minority group of only one I am much too vocal.

C.: To return to the question of the new media, Mr. Stravinsky, won't they offer new resources as well?

I.S.: So one would expect, logically. But I am not convinced that greater resources are what is needed. It seems to me that the possibilities are already rich enough, or too rich. A good artist will not be stopped by a want of resources, which are in the man himself, in any case, and which time makes new every day. The so-called crisis of means is interior.

C.: Lévi-Strauss remarked recently that 'if electronic musicians sought to understand what music is instead of trying to produce it, we would make tremendous progress toward solving the problem which music sets the science of man.'

I.S.: The 'electronic musicians' I know are quite unconcerned about the nature of music, and they would never dare to turn to the philosophy and science of what they are doing, instead of just doing it, definitions of art being not only of no use to artists, but possibly some encumbrance. I expect in my own case that when the computer has quantified my musical characteristics, I will try to avoid them; and though I think I can survive the exposure, I certainly do not welcome it. Lévi-Strauss's inquiries should be supported to the full, nevertheless. He is the first major philosopher to have understood that the true position of music is at the centre of human culture.

C.: Do you agree with Messiaen that 'Nature' (he writes it in upper-case)—its sounds, colours, forms, rhythms—is the composer's supreme resource?

I.S.: Only if you allow the word the scope of the small 'n': the large one signifies no more than a countryside or landscape, personal, perhaps, but not new in kind. In fact, Messiaen's *oiseaux exotiques* differ only in genus, not in musical intention, from Beethoven's homely cuckoo. I do not deny the legitimacy of Messiaen's imitations, of course, or the fertility, to him, of 'natural' resources. What I do say is that no matter how faithful, these imitations are necessarily expressed in, cannot escape being contained by, the harmony, rhythm, instrumental colour, and (especially in Messiaen's case) volume of the contemporary musical language.

C.: Do you think of 'art' and 'nature' as two realities, Mr. Stravinsky, and is there any act of transformation of the one in the other?

I.S.: There are any number of realities, dualisms, pluralisms; concepts of this sort can be set up merely by installing the convincing word-furniture in the available empty idea-flat. For me, music is reality, as I have said before, and like Baudelaire, but unlike Messiaen, '*J'aime mieux une boîte à musique qu'un rossignol.*' As for transformation, I do not admit the idea because I am unable to understand what the cognates would be. Obviously the phenomenal world is refractable in music, or represented in it. The point is simply that I don't understand the mirroring (or the transforming) chemistry. (Try Lévi-Strauss.) It must also be obvious that the composer in me has been partly formed by interactions of choice with the phenomenal world; and obvious that the entelechy of these choices has made me different from other composers. But my picture of the phenomenal world, as a citizen if not as an artist, does not differ essentially from that of other scientific illiterates; or let us say that the differences are comprehensive and that the resemblances conform in enough gritty facts (as they say) to permit the establishment of a statistical society—to return to our starting point.

C.: What do you think of the so-called Age War, Mr. Stravinsky?

I.S.: I admire the long-haired ephebes, though I'm much too square myself to belong to their Big Daddy elect. But are the causes of the Age War so very new? Haven't old people always tended to see too absolutely and too moralistically, and haven't they always narrowed every issue to their own ever-shortening sight? And haven't they—we—always been puzzled by the enthusiasms of the young for things that we have outgrown; and no less puzzled by their lack of sympathy for things that we continue to feel enthusiastic about but that the *times* have outgrown? Whatever the answers, I wonder if any aged person has voiced the feelings of the old more honestly than Tolstoy. I have lately come across a remark of his in Anatol Koni's memoirs (*Vospominaniya O Pisatiliach*, Leningrad, 1965) that, I confess, speaks for me as well: 'Old people dislike the fact that young people talk so much and seem to know so much without having had their experience.'

C.: Generally, as well as in your own case, Mr. Stravinsky, is it more difficult to compose music now than ever before?

I.S.: It is certainly more difficult now, and it always was. As for myself, I can say that ideas seem to come as fluently as ever, and that my new opus may have required less composing time than comparable lengths of music a decade ago. But length is no measurement, nor is the circumstance that the new opus promises to be the most easily digestible of all my recent music; it was *not* easier to compose, I can assure you, and the difficulties in manipulating two series were sometimes extremely inconvenient. At the same time, as the form is that of a *retablo* of small panels, rather than a large-scale fresco, I did not have to carry the burden of a large plan about with me but could work in small doses and tap my 'inspiration'—which is portable, whatever else it may be—only when it seemed full. But I am able to appraise music, while I compose it, only on a technical level: I am an expert but not an evaluator of my functioning mind.

C.: Have other composers written music of value at your age, Mr. Stravinsky?

I.S.: Schütz's *Requiem* surpasses mine by four years, and Richard Strauss was a year older when he wrote his last songs. But your wording implies that *my* music has value, and grateful as I am for the confidence, I cannot participate in judgments of that sort (which does *not* mean that I am willing to entrust them to a Winthrop Sargent or a Professor Auld Lang Syne); my self-auscultations, as I have just said, are reliable, if at all, only as expertise. I warn you, though, that men of my age are vain of their hoard of years, and thirstier for the meeds of praise than they will admit. They like to see themselves as the very end of culture, too, and to dramatize themselves as the 'last defenders' of true art. Their tone, furthermore, often seems to suggest that their own passing will bring on a winter of Pleistocene duration. I have nurtured some such stage conception, I confess, and with a large Lear-like part for myself, 'the last composer who does it all alone, without an orchestrator and even without a computer.' But a beware to anyone else who sees me that way, or implies that, like Lear, I may already have gone 'crackers.' There may be a song or two yet to come before the one which will be called my 'swan.'

WORKING NOTES FOR 'THE FLOOD'

Stravinsky and Balanchine
Hollywood, March 15–16 and April 11–12, 1962

(1) Vacuum. Black scrim. The Prelude music is associated with Chaos, and at the end of the work with Sin. The 12/4 measure is a musical Jacob's Ladder. As we follow it upward the black velvet ceiling opens up. Movements of clouds. Angels' wings fill the screen. The angels are Seraphim, Russian-style, and we are aware of their wings rather than of bodies or faces. The camera pulls downward and we discover that they are framed like icons, and that together they form a triangular altar. I.S.: 'This iconostasis should resemble a real Byzantine altar with the Chiasma or X symbol on top. The piece begins and ends in the Church.' The revelation of the iconostasis must be synchronized with the unfolding of the *Noces*-like Te Deum which is (I.S.) 'not Gregorian but Igorian chant.' The voices should sound at measure 8 as though heralding from a great distance, and from there to measure 46, the musical climax, they should gradually move closer. At measure 46 the screen is filled with a 'celestial effulgence' that washes out all detail.

I.S.: 'To me the Noah story is symbolic, and I think of Noah as an Old Testament Christ figura (Auerbach's sense) like Melchizedek. The subject of *The Flood* is not the Noah story, however, but Sin. Whereas the music of *Petrushka* attempted to create resemblances, *The Flood* music is, structurally speaking, all symbolic.'

(2) The fade-out from the iconostasis begins at measure 60. I.S.: 'The two chords are a signal of approval of what the chorus has been singing.' The Genesis recitative could be accompanied by a montage of pictures symbolizing the Creation. For instance, at the

words, 'Let the dry earth appear' we might see photographs of the moon, of the sea, of deserts. I.S.: 'This is the place for animation and graphic arts, except that I would rather stay away from the surface of the screen.' G.B. has an idea for a hand ballet of rubber sheets and plastic water bags manipulated to suggest shapes and forms. 'But we might also show structures of roots and bones, *à la* Tchelitchev, and of hands sprouting grass from the fingers.'

(3) The recitative becomes an *arioso* at measure 68. This should be danced by one or perhaps several people representing not humans, but non-associated movements, or exploratory movements, or the flexing movements of any living creature's discovery of its body. This section should be thought of as choreographic relief to the purely pictorial recitative.

(4) God, at His first vocal entrance, is represented by unbounded space and crystalline light. The divine rays could be plastic tubing. G.B.: 'A shower of gold dust might fall on the screen every time God sings, but God is the most difficult visualization of all since He is still an object of some curiosity. We might see two ellipses, a parallel to the two voices, breathing or pulsating—the halved ellipses is the divine ideogram, after all—or we might be shown an eye, embryo, or vortex.' I.S.: 'God's music is sometimes reminiscent of Shadow's music in *The Rake*, which should prove, if proof were needed, that musical identities are purely circumstantial.' The audience must think that it is looking up every time God sings. The introductory bass drum notes are a signal for the screen ceiling to open and reveal the divine rays (*i.e.*, plastic tubing).

The Creation of Man. Two shapes, recognizably human though covered, are seen from above. The substance of their chrysalis is peeled from them like two onions, and they stand statuesquely still until the Exile from Eden, at which time they lose their God-like postures. The two shapes are seen in profile only, or only from behind, though (G.B.) 'profiles are unclear in TV and space is as undefined as soup.'

(5) At first, and as God names him, Lucifer, too, stands like a statue. He is perched at a great eminence, and our view is from below. His face is jewelled, and gold wires crop from his head. His costume, glittering with reflective metals, is set off by a

baffle of sequins. G.B.: 'Perhaps we should see a mirror of him, or hall of mirrors with prismatic effects, rather than himself full face.'

(6) With the recitative 'Lucifer was vain,' the Lucifer dancer begins to move. He jumps to a higher rock with each chord, but misses the last one, and at measure 130, the *arioso*, is at floor level dancing a lithe, athletic 'twist.' G.B.: 'The floor is everything in television—backgrounds are comparatively unimportant—and if the floor is wrong, a small-scale hop may look as high as the Eiffel Tower.'

Lucifer's transformation begins at measure 146. Photographically speaking, Satan is Lucifer's negative polarity. What was white becomes black, and the lips turn dark 'red.' The mask shrinks to skull size and becomes a corruption of its former features. The wings grow hideously veined, like a bat's. A short pause at the end of measure 151 will suffice for camera tricks to create sensations of pinwheeling, of falling, and turning upside down. If it were a Cocteau film, Satan would do a parachute jump. The Fall might also be symbolized pictorially, for example, by photographing the tracings on a plate when two atoms collide. Each word of the phrase 'Out, out, horror, helpless, hot, hot, hot' could be projected from a greater distance, and echoed and spiralled by tape reverberation. I.S.: 'Though The Fall is instantaneous, theologically speaking, we must allow enough clock time for the audience to feel the heat.'

(7) Satan's is a sibilant-sweet voice wholly different from the trumpeting Lucifer. I.S.: 'The audience should be able to locate HEAVEN/EARTH/HELL by established camera levels, and recurrent visual clues, as well as by musical distance, which is to say that the music associated with these three spheres ought to be recorded to fixed and recognizably differentiated distances.' Satan's aria 'God made the world for love' is to be sung moderately *forte*, but the parenthetical words with the rhythm from 'The Maidens Came' must be performed *sotto voce*, and the singer should pant and hiss for breath after each dotted quarter-note. The Satan dancer could sit during this aria, and stand at 'to Paradise,' which, incidentally, may be spoken by the narrator if the stage director prefers. We see Satan next in a transparent moth-bag 'serpent' reticulated with wicker rings. I.S.: 'The vermicular disguise must have an excre-

mental shape, and Satan must appear unchanged and plainly visible inside.' The next narration begins before the music, and the Pantomime, for musical continuity, could come between the first two phrases of horn music. I.S.: 'The Tarnhelm music for two muted horns is likely to be my first and last attempt to compose a belly dance.'

(8) Instead of showing the serpent in the tree or coiled about the trunk of the tree, we might see the tree itself turn into serpentine limbs that embrace Eve and Adam. The tree should be light in colour at first, and artistically 'beautiful'—G.B. thinks it should look like a willow, in spite of the fame of its fruit—but as the fruit is plucked, the tree withers and becomes sinister. Eve need not actually pick fruit, of course, but some brief symbolic pantomime —the music allows only a few seconds—should be synchronized with the narrated description. The first 'cursed' should be timed to occur just before the brass chord at measure 177, and the second to just before the second brass chord. With the first note of the contrabassoon, Adam and Eve start to cover themselves with black leaves from the now blackened tree and to walk in shame from Eden. I.S.: 'The allegory of Eden, the curse of Original Sin, in this single measure of music, the largest and most complete-in-itself I have ever composed, is the dramatic climax of the whole work.'

I.S.: 'After Evil, God. At measure 179, the return to the Jacob's Ladder music, the purifying sky leads us to primal light. Air, clouds, distance. I have allotted but fifteen seconds of music for this change from the lowest to the highest, but the music should be able to accomplish it.'

In the God/Noah scene, God's voice may be identified with abstract patterns of light. During God's aria, the camera discovers a black mote far below. We spiral down to it and discover Noah, who must seem to be very small and humble, even at earth level. He wears a patriarch's toga and a tulle cape that rises behind him magically and flickers with light during the tremolos accompanying his speeches to God. The dancing members of his family wear white leotards, and all of them are masked larger than life in slant-eyed masks seen in profile rather than full-face. G.B.: 'We must avoid the question of style, of Biblical, Medieval, Renaissance, Byzantine, or anything else. We know only that we are trying to do something new and without a name.'

WORKING NOTES FOR 'THE FLOOD'

God, or—as we do not actually see Him—His Master's Voice, is a Person, but a Person free of what talent scouts call personality. He is, in fact, a divine bore. Lucifer/Satan, on the other hand, is not a Person, so he abounds in personality. Lucifer/Satan is different each time he sings. In private life he might be an orchestra conductor, a coryphée, a high-diving champion, a film star, an ex-astronaut.

(9) G.B.: 'The God-Noah dialogue could be seen like a tennis game, back and forth from the earth-level view of Noah to the light of the iconostasis, which is the visual anchor throughout *The Flood*. Generally speaking, the audience's view up to this point has been from above, but we now see Noah from, as nearly as possible, his own position. I would like to elevate the dancers to audience eye level by means of a platform, not only because dancers should not be shown from above, but also because the audience should identify itself with the Noah family. Up to this point *The Flood* may seem to have been a spatial fantasy, a myth, a limbo of symbols. Now it is brought down to humanly tilled earth.'

(10) Until the actual Building of the Ark, Noah is alone. He talks to God like a man on a desert island, bows before Him, shields himself from His light. The drum roll will allow time for each visual switch to God, whose Light is immediate, but Noah's speeches begin slowly and falteringly, and his voice is that of an old man. The *ponticello* effect identified with God's radiance also could be used to follow a trajectory of light between God and Noah.

(11) After God's speech, and before measure 247, Noah prostrates himself, hugging the ground. I.S.: 'As all Biblical Hebrews were, so must Noah have been frightened of the sea. The Flood was a more terrible form of catastrophe to a Hebrew farmer, in any case, than it would have been to a Homeric Greek.' At measure 247 we see the legs of his approaching 'bairns.' The legs kneel to him, and we know that he has been lifted up. In the following two measures the dancers stand like an assembly line.

The Building of the Ark. G.B.: 'The dancers' movements must be as mechanical as a watch, and the builders' arms should work like semaphores.' Noah reappears in the coda, measures 328–334, to survey the completed work. The builders stand by to inspect the

Ark, verify its solidity, pinch it to see if it is 'pukka.' I.S.: 'We should not be shown anything of the object itself except, perhaps, a shadow. The Ark is as unreal as the Trojan Horse.'

(12) *The Catalogue of the Animals.* During the loading, Noah's sons stand by like longshoremen. Noah speaks slowly, and before the music begins, but the narrator reads his verse as fast as he is able. The narrator could have a comb-and-tissue-paper, or Jew's-harp, timbre and an American accent, like a square-dance caller or a tobacco auctioneer. G.B.: 'The animals could be shown skiagraphically, as ominously large background silhouettes, but this probably requires animation. Or toy animals and wooden miniatures could be shown looming towards the audience on three conveyor belts (left, right, centre, overhead); and if not toy animals, then photographs of real ones, or representative stylized parts, tusks, humps, splayed or padded feet, zebras' stripes, tails, manes, trunks, wings, though this, too, implies the participation of graphic arts. Rapid changes in camera angles might be exploited also, thus suddenly showing the animals from above or below, or about to tread on us full-face. The birds wing aboard lightly and last, for they can fly to their roosts when we are already flooded. Another notion to consider is that if the animals are miniatures, Noah's sons could stand by the conveyor belts, pick them up and throw them into the Ark—the surface of the screen, the audience's lap—like children heaping toys in a basket.'

(13) *The Comedy.* Noah's wife could be characterized as a Xantippe with a bottle. She has disregarded the Ark when it was building, and she is on her way to a pub when the flood begins. At the last minute her sons—vocally represented by the chorus speaking in unison, or by the narrator—hoist their kicking mother and carry her into the Ark.

(14) I.S. thinks the music for Noah's 'the earth is overflowed with flood' might be supplemented by an electronic effect suggesting 'atmospheric disturbances, or by a pure noise, like a sinus tone.'

(15) The flood is framed at both ends by 'lightning.' Measure 427, the musical turn-around, should mark the climax of the storm visually, but the music is without climax. I.S.: 'The music imitates not waves and winds, but time. The interruptions in the violin/flute line say: "No, it isn't over." As the skin of the sun is fire, so

here the violins and flutes are the skin drawn over the body of the sound. This "*La Mer*" has no "*de l'aube à midi*" but only a time experience of something that is terrible and that lasts.'

G.B.: 'I imagine a floor covered with a shiny bitumen-like material, a deliquescent black surface bubbling like an oil field. Underneath this black tent the male dancers bob up and down from their knees, here and there and all over the camera area, like furuncles. The movements of the dancers might also be synchronized with countervailing explosions of black rubber tubes, balloons, bubble gum. The female dancers move among the mounting and bursting blobs of black. The men are the waves and the women the people drowning in them. The men fling and twirl the women, then swallow them in the folds of their black substance. The audience should feel that *it* is drowning. The audience is definitely *not* on the Ark.'

(16) *The Covenant of the Rainbow*. The colour change in God's music must be compounded with a change in visual 'colour.' G.B.: 'The rainbow could be formed by the dancers, but the result might look like an advertisement for Radio City. Their costumes can help to suggest an arc or a bridge.' At the end of the rainbow stands Noah, bowed in gratitude. Then, directly in front of him, unpleasant black objects (the viewer suspects that he has the DT's) inch out of the ground. They are the wing tips of Satan, another and unexpected survivor of the flood. The mayhem music of the Prelude is repeated to accompany this vision.[1] I.S.: 'As Satan's falsetto aria with flutes is a prolepsis of Christianity, Satan must now be shown as Anti-Christ.' G.B.: 'If Satan is represented as a human-shaped spider in a web when he sings his "God made the world for love," he should be shown here as a creature with no face, or a face with lips but no other features.' Adam and Eve appear again, fleetingly, in the background or in shadow. During the narrator's last speech, the camera dissolves from the allegorical tableau. Satan's final gesture toward Adam and Eve means that 'the affair' is continual and that the end of it is also a beginning. The camera dollies to the iconostasis.

---

[1] This was George Balanchine's idea. It is the second instance in which the choreographer has affected the final shape of a work by Stravinsky: Balanchine induced the composer to extend the return of the F major string music in the *pas de deux* from *Orpheus*. (R.C.)

I.S.: 'Satan's post-diluvian voice exposes a new temperament. Quieter now and very sure of himself, he is inclined to take his position for granted, which is why true Christians may overcome him. In short he seems only to be as ineradicable as the music critic to whose position in the theology of Creation he may be compared. His threat is pedantic and the words are a turgid tirade, but the meaning of the piece is in them. At the end he skips across the stage, far below or out of sight, like the Duke at the end of *Rigoletto*. The camera fades from the angelic choir, and as the music returns to the Jacob's Ladder of the Prelude, 'eternal radiance'—which is different from ordinary TV static—suffuses the screen.'

(17) I.S.: 'Television should some day succeed in sponsoring a new, in the sense of more concentrated, musico-dramatic form (not "instant music drama," which it already has, and which is obtained by pouring water on real composers' ideas). Visually it offers every advantage over stage opera, but the saving of musical time interests me more than anything visual. This new musical economy was the one specific of the medium guiding my conception of *The Flood*. Because the succession of visualizations can be instantaneous, the composer may dispense with the afflatus of overtures, connecting episodes, curtain music. I have used only one or two notes to punctuate each stage in The Creation, for example, and so far I have not been able to imagine the work on the operatic stage because the musical speed is so uniquely cinematographic.

'Other than the possible development of a new musico-dramatic form, the musical life of television does not interest me. A televised concert is a great bore. One sees conductors groomed like English sheep dogs. One sees the timpani and the trombone and the oboe individually. One watches the players breathe, and moisten their embouchures. But seeing individual musicians play, in this way, distracts me, at any rate, from listening to the whole ensemble.

'The so-called underscoring of a TV drama could interest only that composer whose ambition is to design musical wallpaper. In Tahiti, four months ago, a fair native who had never heard European music asked me what my music was "like." Did it resemble Tahitian music—drums—or the jukebox bands in Tahitian night clubs? Our only common ground should have been the music of films we had both seen, but the fair *taïtienne* had never noticed any music in any film. And that should be the underscorers' motto: keep the film viewer from noticing the music, and in the event that he does notice it, help him to forget it as soon as possible.

'As to the question of mass media, I can only say that "the intellectual élite"—if one exists, and I hope it does, history being a cemetery of aristocracies, as Pareto said—the élite is not opposed to mass media, but only to those who seek to determine what is suitable for mass media.

'The question of the parity between visual and musical experience is not altered by television, but nevertheless, if I live to write another opera, I suspect that it will be for the electronic glass tube and the Idiot Box, rather than for the early Baroque stages of the world's present-day opera houses.'

With my son Soulima, on the *Cap Arcona*, June 16, 1936.

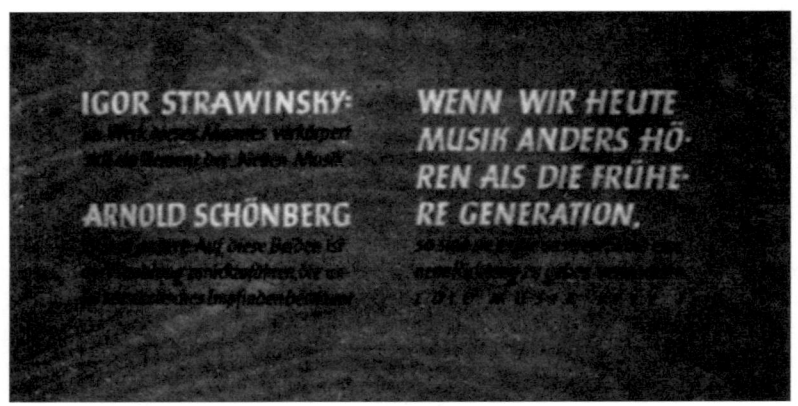

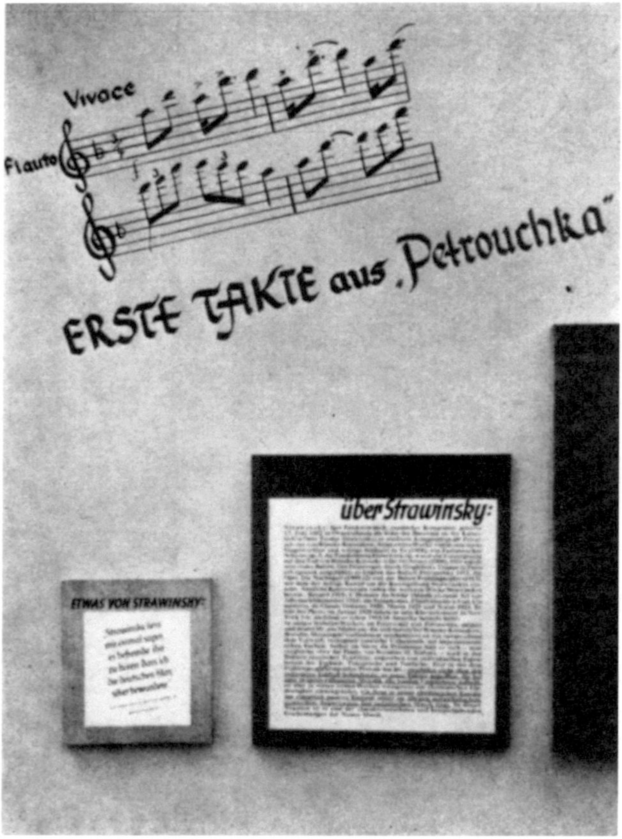

Two photographs of the Dusseldorf Exhibition of Decadent Music, 1938.

STRAVINSKY REVIEWS 'THE RITE'

Three Types of Spring Fever

A Review of Recent Recordings of *Le Sacre du printemps*[1]

'Praises of the unworthy are felt by ardent minds as robberies of the deserving' ... Coleridge

	Berlin Philharmoniker Conductor: H. von Karajan Deutsche Grammophon Gesellschaft	Orchestre National de la R.T.F. Conductor: P. Boulez Internationale Guilde du disque	Moscow State Symphony Orchestra Conductor: P. Kpaat Amalgamated Unions Gramophone Studio
1. Introduction	A *ritardando* has been substituted for the written *accelerando* in measures 5–6 and the differentiation of *tempo primo* and *tempo secondo*, if any, is imperceptible to me. The triplet, five before **13**, is too slow. As a whole the performance is too bland, well blended, sustained: phrases overlap where they should contrast.	The bassoon playing is beautiful and effortless but too saxophone-like and vibrato-shiny, and the second *fermata* in the first measure is too long. The diminuendo to **8** is expertly done, but the oboe should play *staccato* at **9**, and the trumpet *ditto* before **11**. The tempo at the return of the bassoon solo ignores the written *tempo primo*—i.e., it is too fast.	The beginning is unpropitious; the *tempo primo* is lethargic and the clarinet entrances are desultory. The *più mosso* tempo is good, though, and the trill of violins before **7**, the clarinet triplet before **13**, and the oboe articulation at **9** are better than in the other performances. The orchestral balances in this recorded concert are no match for the other two studio-made and edited performances, but to some extent the disadvantages are offset by the feeling that it is a concert: at the beginning, some rather dim applause and a deafening chorus of nasal and pharyngeal expurgations.

[1] Written in October 1964 for *HI FI-Stereo* magazine, New York, partly out of annoyance with the "useless generalities of most record reviewing." The complete text has been published heretofore only in German, in the *Süddeutsche Zeitung*, Munich, September 1965.

2. *The Augurs of Spring* — The oboe figure at **26** must be played *staccato*. The section from **28** to **30** is too smooth in this performance. At **31** the horn and contra-bassoon are weak and their syncopated notes (like all syncopated notes) need accents. Articulation would alleviate the plodding at **34**.

And this is much too fast, as well as ragged, especially at **15**, at two before **20**, and again at two before **21** where the strings are doubtful where to accent. The tuba intonation is muddy before **22**, and from **23** to **28** the tempo is unsteady. The *crescendo* in the trumpets before **29** is unnecessary and unenhancing. More accentuation and acoustical presence from the fourth horn and contra-bassoon would be desirable at **31** and a more controlled tempo is needed at **33**.

The tempo is the best of the three performances, and the steadiest, especially from **31** to **37**. The tuba octave before **22** is more nearly in tune than in the other recordings, and the horn solo at **25** stands out more clearly. I would notate the strumming at **31** differently today, though I am not certain how.

3. *Ritual of Abduction* — The tempo, though very fast, is good except when it *sounds* rushed; I suspect it was facilitated by rebarring, but no matter. An important fault is the equalization of the 2/4 and 6/8 measures toward the end. The eighths, not the measures, should have the same value.

This is slower than the Karajan recording, and it slows still more before **44**. The 2/4 measure nine before **48** is too long, and the quarter-notes in all of the 2/4 measures are *ditto*.

This is generally more distinct than the other recordings, but the horn at **44** is too remote and cavernous.

	Berlin Philharmoniker	Orchestre National de la R.T.F.	Moscow State Symphony Orchestra
4. Spring Rounds	The bass clarinets and their pizzicato doublings are weak at the beginning. Six measures before **54** the orchestral balance is brutally violated by the trumpets, and at **54** the metronomic 160 is slower than the metronomic 132 in the *Ritual of Abduction*.	The *ritardandos* before **49** and **57** are ugly solecisms. I prefer more separation between the quarter-notes of the violas three after **50**, but however that may be, the silting *sostenuto* at **53** is definitely wrong. The downbeat at **55** is ragged.	This errs at the other extreme from the Boulez: there is too much separation between the quarter notes, but they are the right length at **53**.
5. Ritual of the Rival Tribes	The tempo falters in the first measure, but a more disturbing fault is the lack of *staccato* articulation. The daggers over the notes three before **61** should be applied throughout this section: they call for an exaggerated sharpness. Thereafter the eighths are crisply and admirably played. At **66** and *passim* the horns are overbalanced.	The brass chords in the 3/2 measures are too short and the raggedness at **61** and *passim* is disturbing. At **65** and *passim* the horns are too puny, the bass drum and tubas too robust.	The first tuba drags at **57**, and the dynamics are uncertain at two before **59**. The section from **61** to **62** is strangely and inappropriately lyrical here, but the trombone trills before **64** are very satisfying (the Russian instruments were valved), and *ditto* the animal ruttishness of the tubas at **66**. The rhythm, alas, is soggy.

6. *Procession of the Sage*	The trumpets at **70–71** stand out a decibel or so *au-dessus de la mêlée*, and I do mean *mêlée*.	The oboes are too close to the microphone at **68** and the centre of the stage is thus occupied by a detail. The rhythmic polyphony and the orchestral balances at **70–71** are marvellously clear.	The polyphony at **70** is clear enough but the balances are better in the Boulez recording.
7. *The Sage*	The string chord is not properly balanced, the higher instruments being too close to the microphone.	This is more than twice too fast: if there were an Olympic Game for speedy conductors... No, I had not yet heard the head-chopping music in *Salome* when this passage was written.	The tempo is correct but the string chord does not balance; I would write it with a *szforzando* now.
8. *Dance of the Earth*	The gratuitous *accelerando* weakens the build-up in the music. Because of it, too, or partly because of it, the final chord is a shambles.	The bass clarinet is too directly 'on mike' at **75**, and at **78** the basses and tubas are too far 'off'. Though it may be dangerous to say so, a slightly faster tempo than the metronomic 168 would not be amiss: it is not an *allegro*, after all, but a *prestissimo*.	This is the best and most exciting tempo of the three recordings, and the *Hauptstimme* at **75** is, as it should be, in the violas. The strings are clearer than in the other two performances, thanks to articulation.

	Berlin Philharmoniker	Orchestre National de la R.T.F.	Moscow State Symphony Orchestra
9. Introduction	I seem to hear a cricket at the beginning; added natural atmosphere? Is the sleepy tempo also the result of seasonal estivations? The basses are weaker than the other strings at **84**, and at **85** the *piano* of the horns is a *forte* compared to the *piano* of the trumpets at **86**. The changes of tempo at **89, 90**—	This is too hurried, besides which the second trumpet after **84** is too discreet. The solo cellist swoops before **91** as though he were in sympathy with Saint-Säens.	This is also the best string balance for the section beginning at **84**, and the best balance of the two trumpets, but tatterdemalion cello entrances mangle the passage at **85**.
10. Mystic Circles of the Young Girls	—and **91** are slight in this performance if they exist at all. The balance at **99** and **100** is perfect, but the level is too loud; the conductor is probably the victim of the recording engineer who, ideally, should be his *alter ego*. The tempo is shaky at the beginning of the second measure of **103**.	The addition of a *ritard.* before **97** contradicts the silent pulsation with which section **97** begins. The horn balance at **99** is poor, and the *fermata* before **101** is not well measured, but a more important fault is that the *accelerando* at **102** should lead up to the second measure of **103**, instead of overshooting it, as here, then being forced to skid back to a slower tempo!	The tempo at **97** is too hurried. A premature sally by the first cello at **100** proves how little known this music still is in the Soviet Union where, in fact, the present recording preserves the second performance by a Muscovite orchestra in fifty years. The *accelerando* at **102** is well managed and so is the orchestral haemorrhage at **103**.

11. *Glorification of the Chosen One*	The tempo is good but the notes should be needle sharp. The *molto allargando* before **117** is here played incorrectly as five even beats.	The Karajan performance is steadier, and the rhythm is askew here at one measure before **118**, a hiccup by which offbeats become onbeats.	The tempo is *giusto*.
12. *Evocation of the Ancestors*	This is too slow! The pulsation should be the same as in the preceding piece, the old eighths equalling the new quarters like interlocking wheels.	The tempo is perfect and so is the articulation—	The 'E' in the basses being indistinct, and not only here but as a rule, I amended the part for this performance, making a triplet of the F sharp (up bow), E (down bow), D sharp. In future I would omit the timpani altogether after the first note. The result of these changes to this performance is an unwarranted and unfortunate loss of speed.

13. *Ritual Action of the Ancestors*

Berlin Philharmoniker

Whether or not metronomically correct, this *tempo di hoochie-koochie* is definitely too slow, and at **138** the music is duller than Disney's dying dinosaurs. At **136**, second measure, the notes of the triplet must be separated, not glued together. At **139** the bass trumpet is too feeble for the powerful English horn, and at **140** the clarinet intonation is bad. The *rubato* three measures before **142** is unnecessary and debilitating.

Orchestre National de la R.T.F.

—but *this* is too fast, and the onbeats of the *ostinato* are too loud, especially in the first horn and first violins. The trumpets begin so indecisively at **132** and are so slow to screw up confidence that I suspect they were not certain of being in the right place. I do not like this passage played *legato*, incidentally, though it is printed that way.

Moscow State Symphony Orchestra

I hear peculiar percussion 'happenings' at **131**; someone drop something? someone rehearsing another piece? The trumpet articulation is commendable at **132**, but at **134** trumpets and trombones are too loud for the horns. The balance between bass trumpet and flute-in-G is good at the end of the movement; this little dialogue, together with the clarinet melismas that follow, is the best part of the movement, incidentally, for the dance, long since become a model for film safari music has worn the least well in the score (fie on those horns at **138**). It would be comforting to think that the fault is its easy imitability.

14. *Sacrificial Dance*

The sluggish tempo gives the *coup de grâce* to whatever tension may have survived to this point. At **189** the balance is awry, the first trumpet, among other offenders, being too loud for the trumpet in D.

The tempo is fast but good at the beginning. Then, at **157** and **159** it seems unsuitably fast, and the tension is dissipated as much by it as by Karajan's slow tempo. Incidentally, neither performance shows the slightest regard for the *ictus* accent ($|\begin{smallmatrix}6\\8\end{smallmatrix}\ \gamma\ \overbrace{\smile\smile}^{\ }\ |$). The *accelerando* begins too soon at **165**, the tempo drags at three before **190**, and the orchestra is not always together, as for example at two before **154**.

The timpanist miscounts *ca.* **148** and completes this section ahead and independently of the orchestra, a type of mistake that is another indication of the unfamiliarity of the score to Soviet musicians. The tempo is good and in spite of messiness there is more adrenal excitement than in the other recordings. The second measure of **197**, the pivot of the last section and the change in the rhyme, *does* feel like the turning point in this performance.

Résumé: The recording is generally good, the performance generally odd, though polished in its own way; in fact, too polished, a pet savage rather than a real one. The *sostenuto* style is a principal fault; the lengths of notes are virtually the same here as they would be in Wagner or Brahms, which dampens the energy of the music and

Résumé: First, the recording. The vast dynamic range of *The Rite* is emasculated to what may be called standard recording *mezzo-forte* which, next to the wrapping of every sound in echo-chamber flannel, is one of the more irritating aspects of that horrible industry. Noise itself is 'phatic speech,' and volume is an element, and

Résumé: As the mere tape of a concert neither performance nor engineering can stand comparison to the two edited recordings. But whereas the music sounds French in the French recording, and German in the German, the Russians make it sound Russian, which is just right. (I have no space to explain what I mean by these nationalizations in musical

Berlin Philharmoniker

leaves what rhythmic enunciation there is sounding laboured. But I should have begun by saying that the music is alien to the culture of its performers. Schoenberg recognized it as an assault on the Central European tradition, saying that it made him think of 'those savage black potentates who wear only a cravat and a top hat.' (When told, in 1925, that I had declared his 'twelve-tone system' to be a dead end—a *Sackgasse*—he replied with the pun: '*Es gibt keine sackere Gasse als "Sacre"*.') But I doubt whether *The Rite* can be satisfactorily performed in terms of Herr von Karajan's traditions. I do not mean to imply that he is out of his depths, however, but rather that he is in my shallows —or call them simple concretions and reifications. There are simply no regions for soul-searching in *The Rite of Spring*.

Orchestre National de la R.T.F.

though the mediumizing of sound levels does only negligible damage to some music, it deprives *The Rite* of one of its dimensions; which is why a live performance is a shock even now to anyone who has learned the work from recordings. Second, the performance. It is less good than I had hoped, standards being high for Maître Boulez. One would suppose the music to be his *entrée* too, his very lack of Herr von Karajan's *kultur* being a natural advantage here. Apart from sloppinesses—surprising but of no importance—there are very bad *tempi* and some tasteless alterations, such as the *ritards* already cited. The articulation is generally excellent, and a good antidote to the *D.G.G.* performance.

Moscow State Symphony Orchestra

terms.) Then, too, if *The Rite* is new to the Russian orchestra, it must have sounded like the very battle cry of the sans-culottes to the conservative Socialist audience, a fact that helps to charge the atmosphere, more at least than the smog-charged atmosphere of some of our big cities where it has already become a slick show-piece and where with luck it will receive one rehearsal.

None of the three performances is good enough to be preserved.

SOME PEOPLE

Writers

R.C.: What are your personal recollections of Evelyn Waugh, Gerald Heard, Christopher Isherwood, Aldous Huxley?
I.S.: When I met Mr. Waugh, in New York in February 1949, his popping blue eyes looked upon me as an oddity, and I soon found that the cutting edge in the books was even sharper in the person: he was not an immediately endearing character. I was an admirer of Mr. Waugh's talent for dialogue and the naming of characters (Dr. Kakaphilos, Father Rothschild, S.J.). In person I admired, even while suffering from, the agility with which he caused my remarks to boomerang. But whether Mr. Waugh was disagreeable, or only preposterously arch, I cannot say. Horace Walpole remarks somewhere that the next worst thing to disagreeableness is too-agreeableness. I would reverse the order of preference myself while conceding that on short acquaintance disagreeableness is the greater strain. I addressed Mr. Waugh in French, and he replied that he did not speak the language. (His wife contradicted him charmingly, and was rebuked.) I asked whether he would care for a whisky and was told that 'I do not drink whisky before meals,' stated as a fact I should have known. I made an admiring remark about the Constitution of the United States and was reminded that Mr. Waugh is a Tory. I used the word music and was told that music is physical torment to Mr. Waugh. We talked at length only about United States burial customs, and here Mr. Waugh's impressive technical knowledge led me to believe he was gathering material for a doctorate on mausoleums. (I visited Forest Lawn and the Hollywood Pet Cemetery after reading *The Loved One*, and I esteem the book even more highly after viewing the sources of its inspiration.) At dinner I recommended chicken, but this was a new *gaffe*. 'It's Friday,' Mr. Waugh said. But by the time the meatless meal was over and he had peeled, sucked, and blown a cigar,

the clipped conversation was succeeded by whole sentences of almost amiability. I still much admire Mr. Waugh.

Gerald, Christopher, and Aldous are dear and intimate friends —loved ones, in fact, though not in Mr. Waugh's sense.

Gerald is a virtuoso talker, the most brilliant I have ever Heard, and he *likes* to talk, just as Artur Rubinstein *likes* to play the piano. Wystan Auden, by comparison, fishes, though profoundly, between words, and Aldous is too serenely high in tessitura, and in volume too suavely soft.

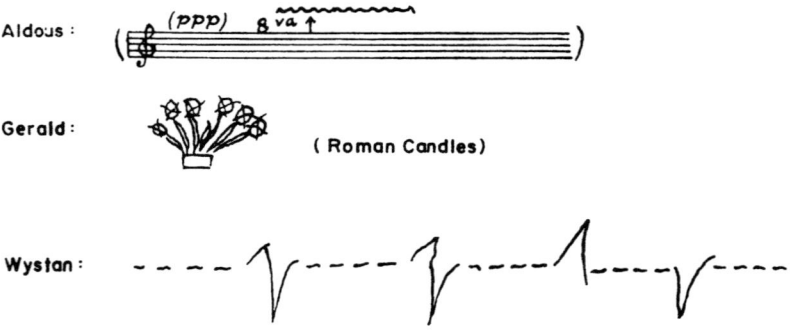

I first saw Gerald lecture in 1950, and regularly, thereafter, attended his Sunday sermons in Hollywood's Ivar Street Temple. He was, all of him, a stunning performer: blue eyes, red beard, long, thin fingers. Especially the fingers. He would grip the sides of the pulpit until the knuckle skin whitened, then flex and spread a skeletal hand. He would direct his index finger aloft in a terrifying gesture of admonishment, then line up four darning-needle digitals from the other hand, and as points one to four were enumerated, strike them down like bowling pins. Before each sermon Gerald would clear the spiritual decks with a minute of meditation and he managed to electrify that minute, too.

I was frightened of him when we first met, of course, and when we dined together after his talks, I ventured hardly a word. At that time I would unkindly think that, though the Guru regarded his listeners intently in the short intervals allowed for reply ('yes' or 'no'), he was in fact already preparing new paragraphs that were not entirely contingent on their answers. Later, when Gerald discovered that I had no idea what his talk was *about*—he used to lead off with questions like 'Have you seen Semov's latest work on the engram complex?' and then go on about the thalamus, which, for all I knew, could have been a vegetable—we relaxed and became the closest friends.

I first heard the name Christopher Isherwood from André Maurois, and I read the Berlin stories on his recommendation. Later, when I knew Isherwood, I was astonished by how exactly like the 'Chris' of the stories he was. The question of (1) 'my art' and (2) 'my life' did not exist for him. His books were himself, and he stepped in and out of them without so much as zipping a zipper.

Everything about Isherwood is boyish: his looks, his laugh, his candour, even the Americanisms—'gee,' 'gosh'—in his speech. His eyes are his most striking feature; they look through you and beyond—all the way up to Karma, in fact. But one also remembers the sharply notched nose, the side-of-the-mouth smile that quickly gives way to full-faced grins, and the high resonant voice, more resonant after alcohol and accompanied then by a marked decline in diction, a peculiar wagging of the knees, and a protrusion of the tongue suggesting that the owner is being garroted. We have often been drunk together—as often as once a week, in the early 1950s, I should think—and in such different climes as Sequoia Park and Santa Monica beach.

On Christopher's first visit to my home, he fell asleep when someone started to play a recording of my music. My affection for him began with that incident. I soon discovered that conversation with him may appear to be relaxed, but is actually full of undertow. 'Serious' conversation, that is; Christopher has a weakness for movieland Hollywood, and about that he can talk without undercurrent trouble. But Christopher is not now, nor ever could have been, a camera. His reflective processes are too agonizingly acute, and however natural his gifts, writing can only be a torture to an intellectual self-awareness of his kind, though of course, a commensurate satisfaction, too. Christopher's intelligence can clear a path of lucidity through even the fuzziest of subjects, and his merciless eye can pierce every disguise of hypocrisy and cant. This much I know from his journals, that Domesday Book in which, I fear, my own sins lie bared. But Christopher is a passionately loyal friend, and I feel very close to him.

Aldous Huxley is the most aristocratic man I have ever known, and I do not mean in the sense of birth, though few people since J. S. Mill can have been so intellectually well bred; or in appearance, though he has a truly noble head. Aldous is an aristocrat of behaviour. He is gentle, humble, courageous, intellectually charitable.

Of the learned people I know, he is the most delectable conversationalist, and of that breed he is one of the few who are always droll. True conversation requires a matching of participants, of course, and though I myself am far from a match for Aldous, I have attended him with equals—his brother Julian, for instance—and come away uplifted from Olympian hours of learning and wit. Julian is a good friend, too, though I have not seen him since 1957 in Totnes, where we listened to Bach's *Aus der Tiefe* together with Arthur Waley, but Julian's is the Other Culture, and though I love to hear him on the joys of eutelegenesis—artificial insemination by an admired donor—his discourse is too recondite for me, and he himself is too much the cynosure of science.

I met Aldous in London at the time of the publication of *Point Counter Point*, through our mutual friend Victoria Ocampo. We saw a film together on that occasion, Tolstoy's *Resurrection*, but concerning Aldous I remember only his strongly lenticular *lunettes* and, through them, his eyes like the magnified eyes of fish in an aquarium. When I saw him next, in Hollywood a dozen years later, the spectacles had disappeared, but he was able to see only by force of mind and by such tricks as memorizing the numbers of steps to his friends' front doors. (I have seen Aldous identify desert flowers from a speeding car, nevertheless, and I know that he discovered an unknown and unsigned Catherwood in a flea market from a distance of twenty feet.) The fact of his weak eyesight undoubtedly accounts for certain of his feats of memory and for his ability to add large sums and solve complex numerical problems 'in his head,' operations he performs with as much velocity and considerably less noise than a Univac robot.

I encountered Aldous only rarely in my first years in California —at that time, the period of *The Perennial Philosophy*, he lived in the desert—but we did exchange letters. Then, in the summer of 1949, we began to meet and lunch together at the Farmer's Market as often as three times a week. We also attended concerts, plays, and film previews, and explored Southern California's museums, zoological gardens, architectural oddities. I remember Aldous in an art gallery diagnosing through his magnifying glass the pituitary disease of a stoatish, school-of-Brueghel peasant. I remember him in the San Diego Zoo referring to each caged creature by its Latin name, while revealing fascinating facts about its sexual habits and I.Q. I remember him peering at a huge Los Angeles bank in construction next to a tiny church and murmuring something about 'God and Mammon in the usual proportion.'

Aldous' 'point-of-view' is more nearly 'synoptic' than that of anyone else I know, and he is my only friend who is equally at home in either Culture. In his home I have met hypnotists, economists, parasitologists, speleologists, industrialists, physicists, occultists (the Lebanese magician, Tara Bey), holy men from India, actors, anthropologists, educators (Robert Hutchins), astronomers (the late Edwin Hubble), and even an occasional literary gent.

What is Aldous 'like'? Well, he is 'like' Beerbohm's willowy drawing, especially the long, ever folding and unfolding legs. He is passionate about music. He is morbidly shy. He cannot resist new gadgets, whether "spiritual" ones like LSD or physical such as the vibrating chair in his study which relaxes me about as much as would a raft ride in the English Channel. Other Aldine characteristics are the tendency to lip-smack over the short, black future of the human race and the little expressions of shock at each day's discovery of each new example of human genius and/or bestiality ('One doesn't know what to think... The mind boggles... Absolutely extraordinary...'). Aldous addresses everyone with the same gentleness, and he always assumes that other people possess as much knowledge and intelligence as himself; whether considering the history of the Baptist Church in Burma or Stendhal's recipe for *zabaglione*, Aldous assumes that you know all this, even though, momentarily, you may have forgotten—which is the Socratic method, after all. But in spite of twenty-five years in Southern California, he remains an English gentleman for whom the ultimate and most wanton demonstration of affection for an old friend is a pat on the shoulder. The scientist's habit of examining everything from every side and of turning everything upside down and inside out is also characteristic of Aldous. I remember him leafing through a copy of *Transition*, reading a poem in it, looking again at the title of the magazine, reflecting for a moment, then saying, 'backwards it spells NO IT ISN(T) ART.'

A decade ago Aldous' friendship was a great comfort to me. And more; Aldous is a healer, a skilful masseur who cured me of insomnia. Since then Aldous has suffered the tragic loss of his wife, Maria. He has also suffered from a Hollywood fire that destroyed his home and all its contents, including his journal about D. H. Lawrence, that more emotionally combustible man than Aldous who, I think, was the one human being Aldous completely admired. But Aldous is an aristocrat, as I have said, and therefore a stoic, and stoicism takes an inward toll. The day after the conflagration, Aldous' only comment was: 'Well, you know, it *is* inconvenient.'

Aldous once introduced a catalogue of my wife's paintings. I quote it both out of family pride and because it contains Aldous' finest qualities:

'Fantasy in painting is of many kinds and runs the whole gamut, from dramatic and symbolic imagination at one end of the scale to purely formal imagination at the other. The imagination which animates Vera de Bosset's work lies somewhere between the two extremes and partakes, in some measure, of both. At the formal end of the scale, she possesses a wonderful gift for inventing coloured patterns; but this gift is combined with another, the gift of transforming her formal inventions into an amused and amusing commentary on the realities around her—an oilfield, for example, a fishbowl, a boulevard at night with all its headlamps and neons. She sees the heavenly oddity in things, she is touched by their absurd and pathetic loveliness; and she proceeds to render these aspects of reality, not directly, not in terms of impressions caught on the wing and recorded in calligraphic shorthand, but at one remove, through what may be called their visionary equivalent. This visionary equivalent of the world's preposterous beauties is a specially created universe of flat houses, depthless landscapes, two-dimensional aquariums—a private universe, where the colours glow with preternatural brilliance, where the darks are like lacquer and the lights like so many small apocalypses from another world of angelic gaiety and paradisal enjoyments. Here is a happy art, and as Jeffrey once ventured to tell Carlyle, "You have no mission on earth (whatever you may fancy) half so important as to be innocently happy." In these paintings Vera de Bosset has certainly done

her duty and fulfilled her mission.'
R.C.: What are your recollections of Cocteau and St.-John Perse?
I.S.: I believe that I first was introduced to Cocteau at a rehearsal of the *Firebird*, but it might have been some time after the *Firebird*, in the street; I remember someone calling my name in the street—'*C'est vous, IgOR?*'—and turning around to see Cocteau introducing himself. In any case, Cocteau was one of my first French friends, and in my first years in Paris we were often together. His conversation was always a highly diverting performance, though at times it was rather like that of a feuilletonist out to make a career. I soon learned to appreciate Cocteau's many sterling qualities, however, and we have remained dear and lifelong friends—indeed, he is the only close friend I have of the *Firebird* period. Just before my first London visit, in the spring of 1912, I moved to the Crillon. I remember that an electric sign in the Crillon lobby flashed reports of Channel weather conditions, and that Diaghilev used to watch for these reports in a perpetual state of alarm. As Cocteau lived nearby, we began to dine together. I remember that we used to frequent a certain café at which stamps were sold as well as drinks and food, and that once when the waiter said '*Cognacs, messieurs?*' Cocteau replied, '*Non, merci, je préfère les timbres.*' In 1914 Cocteau came to Leysin to try to enlist my collaboration in a ballet he proposed to call *David*. A young Swiss artist, Paulet Thévenaz, accompanied him on this trip and painted a portrait of my wife and me. Cocteau's letters to me afterwards are covered with attractive sketches for the never-to-be-realized ballet. But Cocteau is a master designer whose quick eye and economical line can fix the character of any quarry in a few loops. His best caricatures are as good as any but Picasso's, I think, and whereas Picasso's were much modified by erasure, Cocteau scrawled his with photographic speed. When Cocteau first discussed his costumes and masks for the 1952 *Oedipus* with me, he ended each description by scribbling the design on a piece of paper. Though this took him only a few seconds the drawings—I have them still—are each a talented print of his personality.

And his personality is generous and disarmingly simple. Artistically, he is a first-rate critic and a theatrical and cinematographic innovator of a high order. The invention of his that I like best is the angel Heurtebise in *Orphée*. Heurtebise was the name of a well-known elevator company in Paris, and the word thus gave the necessary suggestion of levitation. But Cocteau also made Heurtebise a glazier who carries wing-shaped slats of glass.

Giraudoux, Morand, and St.-John Perse, when I first knew them, were all three employed by the Foreign Ministry (Quai d'Orsay). I was personally closer to Morand than to the others, until the 1939 war, but I was greatly attracted to the theatre of Giraudoux. Giraudoux was the last person I saw in Paris before leaving France in September 1939. I sometimes met him with St.-John Perse, as I met Morand with Edouard Herriot. Perse worked with Briand, and thanks to this connection I was able to obtain permission to travel out of France for concerts when I came to live there, in 1920, which as a depatriated Russian I could not otherwise have done.

I came to know St.-John Perse more closely in his later Washington years, and not only himself, but also his work, and I admire him for the way he has continued to live, with all of his laurels, in that loneliest of cities.

I first read him—the hot Caribbean colours of *Pour fêter une enfance*—in 1911 or 1912. I followed his work thereafter, but at long intervals, which were not my fault, but his. His poems are a doxology of botany, of winds and seas, of stones and earth, of third-person man, and though one should not excerpt from an epic, his epics are temptingly full of memorable lines:

La mer elle-même comme une ovation soudaine!

for example, and

un couple d'aigles, depuis hier, tient la Ville sous le charme de ses grandes manières,

which might have been by Rimbaud, and

des jeunes veuves de guerriers, comme de grandes urnes rescellées,

and

nous avons si peu de temps pour naître à cet instant

which reminds me that I must get back to work.

SOME PEOPLE

Composers

R.C.: Were you aware in your St. Petersburg years of the work of such Russian experimental composers as Rebikov, with his wholetone structures, unresolved dissonances, fourths *à la* Schoenberg's *Kammersymphonie*; Gnessin, with his *Sprechgesang*; and Roslavetz, with his 'non-dodecaphonic serial sets'?

I.S.: I was indeed acquainted with the work of these stepping-stone composers and though I did not meet Roslavetz, I was much interested in certain compositions of his that I heard in St. Petersburg. The now so-called serial-set music, such as *Three Compositions for Piano*, was all written after I left Russia, and I have only recently seen it. Roslavetz came from Tchernigov, incidentally, which is near where my father was born; 'Tcherni' means 'black,' and 'gov' means 'soil.' I did not know Rebikov personally, either, but his innovations were familiar to me in my Rimsky-Korsakov years and I much admired at least one of his works, the ballet *Yelka*.

Roslavetz and Rebikov were 'Moscow composers,' but Gnessin was a Petersburg pupil of Rimsky-Korsakov. I knew him well. I do not think his composer's gifts were strong or original—at least, everything of his that I heard sounded perfectly anonymous—but he was the liveliest and most openminded spirit of the Rimsky group (though when I consider that the others were Steinberg, Glazunov, Gretchaninov, and Tcherepnin, the compliment sounds less generous than I intend it to be). Gnessin's *Sprechgesang* was only of passing interest because, unlike Schoenberg's, it did not grow out of a musical necessity. But Gnessin himself was a striking character. He dressed as an Orthodox Hebrew, but at the same time was identified with radically antisectarian political and social views. I once sent him a note, after we had dined together, saying that I was delighted by our 'sympathetic understanding.' He answered me in a surprised and slightly shocked tone saying that he was sorry but I had been mistaken; he had felt no such sympathy. That was typical of Gnessin and, I suppose, it explains why I remember him.

R.C.: What recent composition by an American-born composer has most attracted you?

I.S.: Elliott Carter's Double Concerto, I think, but you would have to know what other music I have heard to evaluate the preference (and Heaven forbid that I should list it; American music will soon need a Ford Foundation for the Suppression of Unpromising Composers) and how frequently I have heard it. One naturally thinks of large-scale pieces, too, such as Sessions' *Theocritus* and Wolpe's Sympony, which I haven't heard; and the symphonies of X and Y and Z, which, alas, I have—they always take the same half-hour to perform and, one supposes, rather less than that to write. I therefore neglect the many excellent smaller examples of—what seems to me anyway—a distinctly American and very lovely pastoral lyricism: Ruggles' *Angels* and *Lilacs*, Babbitt's *The Widow's Lament in Springtime*, Copland's Dickinson songs.

I like the mood of Carter's Concerto, first of all. It is full of newfound good spirits, as his quartets were not. But the success of the piece is owing to the listener's eventual involvement and satisfaction in its form. That the Double Concerto should suggest Berg's towering example in general ways is not surprising, but I hear direct references to the Berg in it, too. (Carter is certainly not a naïve composer, but I think these Berg bits are unknowing.) The passage from 432 (the piano entrance here is one of the finest things in the piece) to 460, and especially the flute at 436 and the bassoon at 441, remind me of the Berg, and the architectural plot of the solo instruments—their roles as alternate soloists, duo soloists, parts of ensemble groups—also is reminiscent of the Berg. (Still another Berg invention is the idea of controlled accelerando and ritard.: the *Monoritmica* in *Lulu*.) The Concerto poses many interesting performance problems, not so much in instrumental technique—not in the wind and string parts anyway, though the percussion is a different matter—as in rhythm. The score introduces no metrical difficulties, and as the proportionalisms of tempos are easy to hear if the orchestras are reversed from the composer's seating plan so that the conductor stands next to the harpsichord, it is easy to conduct. Incidentally, the most effective example of an interlocking of tempos by a held-over beat pattern is precisely where it is most apparent (loudest): the percussion at measures 143–144. I do not think the chief rhythmic difficulty is in the notation—though I can imagine orchestra players complaining about that, and perhaps fidelity to the writing of the rhythmic series does make the instrumental parts momentarily more difficult to read: I mean, for example, four dotted sixteenths to the dotted quarter, according to the Longy-Miquelle system, rather than 'four for three' without the dots, as I would now do it. The rhythmic problem of the Concerto is the old one common to most contemporary music. The player manages the notes, but cannot count the rests or feel irregular pulsations—or regular ones, but without simple patterns—when he is not playing.

I like not only the shape but also the sense of proportion in the Concerto, and I like the harpsichord and piano writing very much, too. And the intended high point, the coda, is the real climax of the piece. This section is unclear in the recording, where the rhythm is a blur and the dynamic plan is without profile. The question of dynamics in recording practice must be criticized more strongly than anyone has criticized it so far. The harpsichord is weak in volume by nature, or so the engineer assumes; but this weakness is overcompensated by about ninety per cent in recording. I cannot comment upon or add to the composer's own analysis, but analysis as little explains a masterpiece or calls it into being as an ontological proof explains or causes the existence of God. There, I have said it. A masterpiece, by an American composer.

R.C.: What are your memories of George Gershwin?

I.S.: I met Gershwin in New York in 1925 and spent an evening with him at Paul Kochanski's. He knew a few words of Russian, but no French, and therefore we had to talk through Kochanski. I remember him as a tall man—taller than I am, anyway—and very nervously energetic. At that time I hardly knew who he was and I was totally unacquainted with his music. He played the *Rhapsody in Blue* for me at the piano that night and some other pieces whose titles I forget, but none of the music interested me. I saw him again in Hollywood shortly before his death, at a dinner given for me by Edward G. Robinson, with Chaplin, Paulette Goddard, Marlene Dietrich. Gershwin was very *à la page* then, but he had not been spoiled.

The popular story about myself and Gershwin regrettably is untrue. Gershwin is supposed to have come to me in Paris and to have asked me how much I would charge to give him lessons. I am then supposed to have asked how much he earned, and after he had supposedly said $100,000 a year, my supposed reply was, 'Then I should take lessons from you.' A nice story, but I heard it about myself from Ravel a year before I met Gershwin. One rather bad moment of pure Gershwin in my own music, incidentally, though it anticipated the Brooklyn composer by a decade, is the Emperor's *'Bonjour à tous'* in *Le Rossignol*.

R.C.: And Hindemith and Křenek. What do you recall of your associations with these composers?

I.S.: I met Hindemith for the first time in Amsterdam, I believe in 1924, at a concert by the Amar Quartet, of which he was the violist. I remember him as short, stocky, and even at that time almost bald. He was already widely discussed as a composer, but I had not heard any of his music, and I am no longer certain which piece of his I did hear first, though I think it might have been the attractive unaccompanied Viola Sonata, opus 11, played by himself. (*'Hindemith kratzt auf seiner Bratsche,'* the Schoenbergians said.) I encountered Hindemith often in the late 1920s but I knew him well only after 1930, when we were both published by Schott, which was then under the guidance of Willy Strecker, who was to become my close friend. Strecker was extremely effective in promoting Hindemith's music after World War I and in advancing the idea of a Stravinsky-Hindemith team. He persuaded me to publish a favourable opinion about Hindemith's *Das Unaufhörliche*, a work I really only thought very appropriately named, just as, years later, he induced me to sign a squib recommending Henze's *Boulevard Solitude*.

In Berlin, one day in 1931, I was invited to the Hindemiths' for lunch, but when I arrived the housekeeper said the esteemed composer and his wife had not yet returned from their daily exercises. Just then they came running up the stairs, both in white linen shorts and both out of breath. They had been trotting in the Grünewald with their athletic instructor and, judging from the panting, they must have run home from there. I think of this incident every time I hear one of those setting-up-exercise concertos by Hindemith, though the whole scene seems as remote to me now as a Berlin story by Isherwood.

Hindemith and I travelled the same concert circuit in the 1930s, and our paths often crossed. We were neighbours for a time in Positano in 1937, when I was composing my Concerto in E flat and he the *St. Francis* ballet, which I heard later that year in Paris. I recall with pleasure an excursion to Paestum which we took together then. Our friendship continued to develop in the United States during World War II, but we saw each other only rarely after the war—at a concert in New York in 1953 in which he conducted his Trakl song-cycle, in Munich at the time of his opera *Harmonie der Welt*, and at Santa Fe in 1961, where he conducted his *Neues vom Tage* and where his wife protected him from the tourists as if he were Rock Hudson.

I am not entitled to an opinion of Hindemith's music, as I know next to nothing of it. I have seen none of his operas and have heard but few examples of his concert music. I did not like *Last Year at Marienleben* but I enjoyed his ballets *The Four Temperaments* and *Hérodiade*, and the *Schwanendreher* when I heard him play it in 1935 or 1936. And I found the *Ludis Tonalis* moderately interesting to look at. But I have also heard pieces of his that were as arid and indigestible as cardboard and as little nourishing. I am ashamed of my ignorance of Hindemith, though, for he was a loyal friend, and a man of elegant conduct and a truly delightful fund of humour.

Křenek was a chubby, cherub-faced young man when he came to call on me in Nice one day in the late 1920s. I knew of him then only as the *Wunderkind* composer of *Jonny spielt auf*. He brought me a gift, a rare orchestra score of a Strauss waltz, and thus began an acquaintance that in our mutual California years was to develop into an affectionate sympathy. I do not remember the exact occasion of our next meeting, but I think it was at one of Klemperer's Bach concerts in Los Angeles or at a small concert honouring Schoenberg's seventy-fifth birthday. We saw each other regularly thereafter, and exchanged visits to each other's homes. Křenek lived in a Kokoschka mountain-landscape in the Tujunga Hills, north of Los Angeles. His dining-room there was decorated with his own Kokoschka-like painting, and his attractive watercolours of desert views hang throughout the house. I knew little of Křenek's music a decade ago, but I knew and liked the Symphonic Elegy for Strings and the *Lamentations of Jeremiah*. Perhaps my own *Threni* shows contact with the *Lamentations*. Křenek's short treatise on twelve-tone counterpoint was the first work I read on that subject, too, and his *Spiritus Intelligentiae Sanctus* was the first electronic 'score' I had an opportunity to study.

Křenek is an intellectual and a composer, a difficult combination to manage, and he is profoundly religious, which goes nicely with the composer side, less easily with the other thing. He is also a gentleman and a scholar—an authority on Offenbach as well as Ockeghem—and that is an even rarer combination, or so I would think, judging from the scholarly journals I read.

Křenek's sixtieth birthday was celebrated recently by the whole musical world—a unit that does not include his adopted city, where he can sometimes be seen conducting for no remuneration at certain interesting small concerts, but never at the 'Philharmonic.' (He should not be unhappy about this though, for to be ignored by the 'Philharmonic' puts him in good company: Schoenberg was totally disregarded by the local orchestra for the whole of his seventeen years in Los Angeles.) But Křenek will be honoured one day even at home, and I look forward to reading Charles Eliot Norton lectures by him on—may I suggest a subject?—'The Psychological Principles of Auditory Form'; something of that sort is needed by a musician, in the line of Ehrenzweig's *Psychoanalysis of Artistic Vision and Hearing.*

R.C.: Have you any further personal recollections of Arnold Schoenberg?

I.S.: I had heard Schoenberg's name as early as 1907, but *Pierrot lunaire* was my first contact with his music.[1] I had not seen any score by him either, and to my recollection nothing by him was played in St. Petersburg while I lived there. I do not know how the Berlin meeting with him came about, but the initiative for it must have been Diaghilev's; Diaghilev hoped to commission Schoenberg. I remember sitting with Schoenberg, his wife Mathilde, and Diaghilev at a performance of *Petrushka*, and I have a clear memory of Schoenberg in his green room after he had conducted the fourth performance of *Pierrot lunaire* in the Choralion-saal, 4 Bellevuestrasse, Sunday, December 8, 1912, at twelve o'clock noon; I still have my cancelled ticket. Albertine Zehme, the *Sprechstimme* artist, wore a pierrot costume and accompanied her epiglottal sounds with a small amount of pantomime. I remember that and the fact that the musicians were seated behind a curtain, but I was too occupied with the copy of the score Schoenberg had given me to notice anything else. I also remember that the audience was quiet and attentive and that I wanted Frau Zehme to be quiet too, so that I could hear the *music*. Diaghilev and I were equally impressed with *Pierrot*, though he dubbed it a product of the *Jugendstil* movement, aesthetically.

I encountered Schoenberg several times during my short stay in

[1] A. I. Siloti's *Vospominaniya I Pisina* (Reminiscences and Letters), Moscow, 1963, mentions an early performance of *Verklärte Nacht* in St. Petersburg that I now remember attending.

Berlin, and I was in his home more than once. I arrived at the Adlon Hotel from Switzerland on November 20, 1912; I remember that I had been working on the orchestra score of *Le Sacre* on the train. Eduard Steuermann, the pianist of the first *Pierrot*, recalls a dinner with me in Schoenberg's house at which Webern and Berg were present but, alas, I have no recollection of this, my First and Last Supper with the hypostatic trinity of twentieth-century music.

When I met Berg in Venice in September 1934, at the concert in which I conducted my *Capriccio* and Scherchen *Der Wein*—two pieces as different as Eros and Agape—we did not mention an earlier meeting. Someone told me that after hearing the *Capriccio*, Berg said he wished he could write 'such light-hearted music,' but when he introduced himself to me in the artists' room after the concert his manner seemed slightly condescending—though short men often feel they have been condescended to by tall men.

Schoenberg was small in stature. I am five feet three inches and weigh 120 pounds. These measurements were exactly the same fifty years ago, but Schoenberg was shorter than I am. He was bald, too, with a wreath of black hair around the rim of his white cranium, like a Japanese actor's mask. He had large ears and a soft, deep voice—not so *basso* as mine—with a mellow, Viennese accent. His eyes were protuberant and explosive, and the whole force of the man was in them. I did not know then what I know now, which is that in the three years prior to *Pierrot*, Schoenberg had written the *Five Pieces for Orchestra*, *Erwartung*, and *Die glückliche Hand*, a body of works we now recognize as the epicentre of the development of our musical language. (By 'we' I mean a small group still, for most composers are still bumping into each other in the dark.) The real wealth of *Pierrot*—sound and substance, for *Pierrot* is the solar plexus as well as the mind of early twentieth-century music—was beyond me as it was beyond all of us at that time, and when Boulez wrote that I had understood it *d'un façon impressioniste*, he was not kind but correct. I *was* aware, nevertheless, that this was the most prescient meeting in my life, though the future is never an idea in one's mind, is never part of one's speculations at such moments. Time does not pass but only *we* pass and I do not know *more* now than I did then, for the quality of my knowledge is different, but I did know and recognize the power of the man and his music at that meeting half a century ago.

Shortly after the performance of *Pierrot*, Schoenberg left for St.

Petersburg to conduct his *Pelleas und Melisande*. We were on good terms at parting, but we never met again. In Morges, in 1919, I received a very cordial letter from him asking for pieces of my chamber music to include in his Vienna concerts 'The Society for Private Performances.' I wrote and he wrote again. Then, in 1920 or 1921, I heard *Pierrot* in Paris, conducted by Darius Milhaud, and performed by Marya Freund. After that, incredibly, I did not hear another note by Schoenberg until the Suite, Opus 29, in Venice in 1937, and the *Prelude to Genesis* in Hollywood in November 1945. At the later occasion we might well have met, for we were in the recording studios on the same day and we sat on opposite sides of the Wilshire Ebell Theater at the première of the *Genesis Suite*. Schoenberg conducted his Serenade in Venice in September 1925, and I played my Piano Sonata there the next day, but neither of us heard the other's music. Years later, when I knew the Serenade, I realized that, as reported to me at the time, Schoenberg probably did like my *Histoire du soldat*. When I came to Los Angeles in 1935, Klemperer and other mutual friends tried to bring us together, but only after 1948 did a meeting seem possible. I saw Schoenberg for the last time in 1949 when he appeared on-stage at a concert and read a delicately ironic speech acknowledging the honour of the freedom of the city of Vienna just conferred on him, a half-century too late, by the Austrian consul. I remember that he repeatedly addressed the consul as 'Excellency' and that he read from large sheets of paper which were extracted one by one from his pocket, his eyesight being very poor then, and each page containing but a few words. Even on such an occasion, instead of an all-Schoenberg programme only the early *Kammersymphonie*[2] was played.

Two days after Schoenberg's death, I happened to visit Mrs. Mahler-Werfel's home and to see there Schoenberg's not-yet-dry death mask. Less than a year later, his *Erwartung* and my *Oedipus*

[2] I admire the *Kammersymphonie*, but am not attracted by the sound of the solo strings—they remind me of the economy-sized movie-theatre orchestras of the 1920s—though I agree that the multiple-string version tames and blunts the piece unduly. At times the *Kammersymphonie* sounds to me like a joint creation of Wagner, Mahler, Brahms, and Strauss, as though one of these composers had written the upper line, one the bass, etc. But the triplets were written not by Brahms, whose triplets are lyrical, but by Mahler, whose triplets are rhetorical. Nevertheless the *Kammersymphonie* is more polyphonic than the music of any of these composers.

Rex—an unthinkable juxtaposition a few years before—were performed together in Paris by the late Hans Rosbaud, as a double bill. I hope Schoenberg would have been pleased. I know I was.

R.C.: Would you comment on the popular notion of Schoenberg and Stravinsky as thesis and antithesis?

I.S.: Like every arbitrary argument, that one is easy to develop, but in terms of large and not very waterproof generalities. For example:

STRAVINSKY:	SCHOENBERG:
1. Reaction against 'German music' or 'German romanticism.' No '*Sehnsucht*,' no '*ausdrucksvoll*.'	'Today I have discovered something which will assure the supremacy of German music for the next hundred years.' Schoenberg, July 1921.
2. Fox (eclectic and abundant variety). (Aron)	Hedgehog. (Moses)
3. 'Music is powerless to express anything at all.'	'Music expresses all that dwells in us . . .'
4. Chief production is of ballets.	'Ballet is not a musical form.'
5. Learns from others, a lifelong need for outside nourishment and a constant confluence with new influences. Never a teacher. No writing about musical theory.	An autodidact. After the early works, no influence from other composers. Also a teacher. Large amount of writing on musical theory. His philosophy of teaching is 'Genius learns only from itself; talent chiefly from others. Genius learns from nature, from its own nature; talent learns from art.'
6. Composes only at the piano.	Never composed at the piano.
7. Composes every day, regularly, like a man with banking hours. Hardly a scrap unfinished or unused.	Composed fitfully, at lightning speed, and in the heat of inspiration. Therefore, many unfinished works.

SOME PEOPLE

STRAVINSKY:	SCHOENBERG:
8. Remote-in-time subjects: *The Rake's Progress*.	Contemporary subjects (protest music): *Survivor from Warsaw*.
9. Metronomic strictness, no *rubato*. Ideal is of mechanical regularity (*Octuor*, Piano Concerto, etc.).	Much use of *rubato*.
10. Diatonicism.	Chromaticism.
11. *Secco*. Scores contain minimum of expression marks.	*Espressivo*. Scores full of expression marks.
12. Prefers spare, two-part counterpoint.	Preferred dense eight-part counterpoint (the choruses, op. 35; the *Genesis Prelude* canon).
13. 'What the Chinese philosopher says cannot be separated from the fact that he says it in Chinese.' (Preoccupation with manner and style.)	'A Chinese philosopher speaks Chinese, but what does he say?' ('What is *style*?')

A parlour game, no more, and in any case the parallelisms are more interesting. For example:

1. The common belief in Divine Authority, the Hebrew God and Biblical mythology, Catholic culture.
2. The success obstacle of the first pieces, *Verklärte Nacht* and *The Firebird*, which remained the most popular of all our works, all our lives and after.
3. The common exile to the same alien culture, in which we wrote some of our best works (his Fourth Quartet, my *Abraham and Isaac*) and in which we are still played far less than in the Europe that exiled us.
4. Both family men and fathers of several children, both hypochondriac, both deeply superstitious.
5. For both of us, numbers are things.
6. Both of us were devoted to The Word, and each wrote some of

his own librettos (*Moses und Aron, Die glückliche Hand, Jacobsleiter, Les Noces, Renard*).
7. Each of us composed for concrete sounds, unlike the later Webern, in which choice of sound is a final stage.
8. For both of us, the row is thematic and we are ultimately less interested in the construction of the row, *per se*, than is Webern.

---

*Sounds may be, and most of those that
we hear are, public objects.**

R.C.: Would you amplify your remarks in *Memories and Commentaries* concerning Edgar Varèse and his music?

I.S.: Varèse himself is so vivid—his electrified hair makes me think of Struwelpeter or the Wizard of Oz—and his words are so concrete that I would rather quote than attempt to describe. One striking phrase of his—'I like a certain awkwardness in a work of art'—reveals more about him than I could in an essay. That is the remark of a humanist (if I can use the word without invoking its overtones of conservatism), and it is the humanist aspect of Varèse which I propose to consider. Varèse has made a new adjustment of the limits between 'human' and 'mechanical,' and not merely theoretically, but by the force of his own humanizing creations. In fact, he has little theory, and in his lifelong crusade to emphasize sound over scheme he has avoided codification and description wherever possible. 'Flowers and vegetables existed before botany,' he says, 'and now that we have entered the realm of pure sound itself we must stop thinking in the frame of twelve tones.' Those of us who have not stopped thinking in that frame he calls '*les pompiers de douze sons.*' Few composers have dedicated themselves with such singularity to the 'purity of sound' ideal, and few have been as sensitive to the totality of sound characteristics.

We are naturally curious about the antecedents of such a man. They are either not apparent or else too apparent, by which I mean that the most obvious of them are likely to appear as solecisms. This is the case with his frequent references to Debussy—at many places in *Amériques*; in measures 73–74, horns and trumpet, in *Déserts*; in the choral melody at No. 12 in *Ecuatorial*, a melody that reappears in *Density 21.5*; and in *Arcana*, at Nos. 13–14, at two

*P. F. Strawson, *Individuals: an Essay in Descriptive Metaphysics.*

measures before No. 20, and at five measures before No. 28, in the trumpets. But Varèse's melodic characteristics, whether lyrical as in the *Offrandes*, or popular as in the marching tunes in *Arcana*, are always Gallic. Perhaps some of *me* peeks through in *Arcana*, too:[3] *Petrushka* at No. 9; *The Firebird* at three measures before No. 5— this, a variant of the first motive of the piece, is what Varèse calls the *idée fixe*, but the real *idée fixe* is the figure of five repeated notes which occurs in nearly all of his music; and *Le Sacre du printemps*, at two measures before No. 17, and one measure before No. 24, and in the section beginning at No. 19. And Varèse's motorized metrical scheme may also owe something to my example. The many changes of tempo in *Arcana* involve, because of metrical proportionalism, few changes of beat. Echoes of the jazz age survive in *Arcana* and *Amériques*, too, though Varèse has eliminated some of them in the revised (1960) version of *Arcana*. (See the original score at Nos. 33–34. The revision cuts repetitions, replaces *tutti* with silence, and avoids the final C major triumph, the musical low point of the original score, but succeeded there by a skilful use of the mediant.)

One learns, at first with surprise, that Varèse is solidly grounded in seventeenth-century music and in 'early' music in general, and that Ingegneri and Goudimel are among his favourite composers. Perhaps this may be attributed to his background as a choral conductor rather than to his formal musical education. By the contretemps of French *fin-de-siècle* birth, Varèse's teachers were d'Indy, Roussel, and Widor. He recalls some of these *barbes* as vividly as I warned he would: '*Ils n'étaient pas simplements des cons, ils étaient des généraux des cons. . . . Ils ont pensé que Marc-Antoine Charpentier avait composé Louise.*' Varèse says that he fled France to escape academic stupidity on the one hand ('*Les professeurs étaient reglés comme du papier à musique*') and the 'vice of intellectualism' on the other.

Varèse has been recognized, but is a lonely figure still. This is partly because he preferred composing to the career of being a composer; and instead of lecturing to ladies' clubs, writing articles on the state of music, participating in symposia, travelling on fellowships, he has remained at home and gone his own way, alone.

I knew of Varèse as a pioneer in the 1920s, and again, with

[3] And perhaps some of him peeks through in my *The Building of the Ark*, and in the use of the gongs in my *Prayer*.

Déserts in the 1950s, as a prophet of 'spatial music.' I sometimes think I understand what he means by sound depth, at least in *Déserts*, in which some of the electronically realized sounds do seem to come from a distance and as though from the ends of spirals, and where presence and distance are apparent structural factors in the composition. But Varèse has achieved other, more obviously tangible things as well: in *Déserts*, a form based on patterns of recurrence and incidence, and a purely intervallic harmonic structure. As an electronically organized and electronically produced sound composition, *Déserts* was possibly the first piece to explore the liaison characteristics between live instrumental music and electronically recorded sound. I refer to the transitions between the four instrumental portions and the three taped segments of electronically organized sound which connect and interpolate them; these transitions, exploiting the border country between the live and the electronically attenuated suggestion of the live, are, I believe, the most valuable development in Varèse's later music.

Varèse was among the first composers to employ dynamics as an integral formal element (the dotted-line sections in the first part of the *Déserts* score), and to plot the intensities of a composition, the highs and lows in pitch, speed, density, rhythmic movement. As Webern is associated with small volumes, so Varèse is identified with large ones. 'Turn it up,' he will say. 'I like it louder.' One thinks, not without sympathy, of the listener who wrote on his programme of the London performance of Haydn's 'Military' Symphony in 1795: 'Grand but very noisy' (H. C. Robbins Landon: *Supplement to the Symphonies of Joseph Haydn*). Now that I have mentioned Webern, I should note that Varèse was aware of Schoenberg and Webern thirty-five years ago, which is to say that he had experienced long ago the now familiar stage fright attending the discovery of how vastly more difficult composition is after those masters.

In the use of percussion and wind instruments, Varèse is an innovator of the first rank. *Déserts* discovers a world of possibilities for the tuba, and Varèse and Schoenberg, between them—Schoenberg in the *Seraphita* song—have created new roles for the trombone. With percussion instruments Varèse's knowledge and skill are unique. He knows them and he knows exactly how to play them. Speaking for myself, I weary of wood blocks and snare drums, but I love the guiro, the gongs, the anvils of *Ionisation*; the thundering metal sheets, the lathes, the *claves* of *Déserts*; the parabolas of siren music that make *Amériques* sound like an old-fashioned air-raid. I also love the scurrilous string drum in *Nocturnal*; the doubling of flute, piccolo, and piano in *Déserts*; and the most extraordinary noise of all, the harp attack ('heart attack,' I almost said, and that is what it almost gives one) at measure 17 in *La Croix du sud*. Varèse's most original large-orchestra sonorities are, I think, in the extreme upper instrumental ranges throughout *Arcana*.

Varèse's music will endure. We know this now because it has dated in the right way. The name is synonymous with a new intensity and a new concretion, and the best things in his music—the first seven measures from No. 16 in *Arcana*, the whole of *Déserts*—are among the better things in contemporary music. More power to this musical Brancusi.

Some Older Composers

R.C.: Will you list some of your favourite events in the symphonies and quartets of Beethoven?[4]

I.S.: The Eighth Symphony is a miracle of growth and development and I am therefore reluctant to cite my particular admirations out of context. Nevertheless, the entrance of the trumpets and drum in F major in the last movement, after the F sharp minor episode, is the most wonderful moment. I actually had the temerity to imitate this in the March that is No. 6 of my Eight Instrumental Miniatures. For me, the Ninth Symphony contains no event of comparable force. But then, for me, nothing in the Ninth is as perennially surprising and delightful as the development section of the last movement of the Fourth Symphony, or the repeated B flat-A in the Trio of the Fourth, or the *tutti*, measures 50–54, in the *Adagio* of the Fourth.

What are my criticisms of the Ninth? Consider the *Adagio* without prejudice—or try to. The echo-dialogue of winds and strings lacks variation, and the *Andante moderato*, with the pedal A and the repeated octaves, sixths, thirds, is harmonically heavy. (The metronome markings must be in error here, incidentally, for the *Adagio molto* is 60 and the *Andante moderato* only 63.) I find the

[4] Stravinsky's 'answer' is a composite of remarks made at my rehearsals of four Beethoven symphonies. The identifying measure numbers were added later.

movement rhythmically monotonous, too—for Beethoven—except in its finest episode, the E flat *Adagio*, but the effect even of that beautiful passage is deadened by the rhythmic inanity of the subsequent 12/8. Another weakness, or miscalculation, is the repetition, after only six measures, of the heroics at measure 121. What has happened to Beethoven's need for variation and development? The movement is the antithesis of true symphonic form.

The failure of the last movement must be attributed, in large measure, to its thumping theme. As the composer cannot develop it—who could?—he spreads it out like a military parade. I am ever surprised in this movement by the poverty of the *Allegro ma non tanto*, as well as by the riches of the *Allegro energico* (especially measures 76–90, which, oddly enough, anticipate Verdi). I am undoubtedly wrong to talk this way about 'The Ninth,' of course, or to question 'what everyone knows.' 'The Ninth' is sacred, and it was already sacred when I first heard it in 1897. I have often wondered why. Can it actually have something to do with a 'message' or with so-called proletarian appeal?

The quartets, in any case, are addressed not to the great unwashed, but to a select few, and the later sonatas speak to an intimate two or three, or perhaps only to the composer himself (the A flat sonata, for example, which might also have been a string quartet and could become one by an adjustment of the ranges). The music of the Opus 59 quartets is always so marvellously sustained and the substance to be sustained is so good that I cannot cite out of context, yet what a stroke is the A flat in measure 266 of Opus 59, number 1, or, in the second movement, what marvels are measures 65–68, 394–404, and 290–294 (on the strength of this last passage alone Beethoven must be considered first among rhythmic innovators). But the last movement of this quartet, the *Kazatchok*, is often badly played because the dotted notes are held too long. For me the most astonishing passages in Opus 59, number 2, are measures 210–226 in the first movement, and measures 64, 79, 84 (the A natural!) in the second movement; one could write a book *Beethoven and the Octave* on this second movement. The *Adagio* is another instance of a piece often destroyed by poor performance: the 16ths that follow dots and rests should be shortened in more places than the three measures in which Beethoven specifies 32nds. The long B flat bass in the last movement is a wonderful surprise, and so is the passage in measures 344–350. In Opus 59, number 3, the *Andante* movement anticipates Schumann and Mendelssohn, neither of whom was capable of anything as original as the *pizzicato* idea itself or as mighty as the upbeat to measure 66 and the great arc from measure 127 to measure 135.

The 'Harp' quartet is slighter than the 'Rasumovskys,' I think, and its final movement, in spite of the sixth variation with the amazing D flat in the cello, breaks the empyrean flight that began with Opus 59, number 1. I seldom listen to the 'Harp' quartet because of the habitual bad performance of it. The *Adagio ma non troppo* is usually played '*troppo*'; and the figure

in the *Presto* sounds in most performances like a sloppy 6/8 or like

because instrumentalists commonly do not cut the dots of the dotted notes. My favourite places in the quartet are measure 110 to the 'harp' episode in the first movement, and the modulation at measures 192–193.

As for the '*Quartetto Serioso*,' the most wonderful event occurs in measures 47–65 of the *Allegretto*.

And the last quartets? Like the greatest beauties, they are a little flawed, and except for Opus 127 and the Great Fugue, each has its *ennuis*. The three final movements of Opus 130 are as pedestrian as anything bearing the stamp of the master, and so are the second 6/8 movement of Opus 131, the first 3/4 movement of Opus 132, the *Lento* movement of Opus 135 (how like Tchaikovsky is the beginning of that movement!). The delights of Opus 132 are, for me, the Schubertian *Allegro appassionato* and the quarter-note canon, which I think Schoenberg may have remembered when he composed the second episode of his String Trio. My particular pleasures in Opus 127 are the modulation in the second movement (measures 75–78); measure 91; measures 97–101; and the whole *presto* of the *Scherzando*, but above all measures 244–270. What I find least attractive in the last quartets is the Ninth-Symphony-style recitative in the finale of Opus 135, in the violin cadenza in Opus

132, and in the *ritenuto* passages in the finale of the music drama, Opus 131.

R.C.: You have often declared your taste for Weber and Mendelssohn, and even avowed a kinship with these composers. When were you first aware of this attraction? And what are your sympathies for Schubert, Schumann, Chopin?

I.S.: Mendelssohn's elegance attracted me early in my career, as my *Scherzo fantastique* indicates, but my appreciation of Weber did not come until the 1920's, with a performance of *Der Freischütz* in Prague conducted by Alexander von Zemlinsky. I acquainted myself with all of Weber's music after that *Freischütz*, with the result that his piano sonatas may have exercised a spell over me at the time I composed my *Capriccio*; a specific rhythmic device in the *Capriccio* may be traced to Weber, at any rate. The Weber of the *Invitation to the Dance*, the overtures, the *Konzertstück*, and the Mendelssohn of the 'Italian' Symphony, the Octet, the *Rondo Capriccioso*, and other piano pieces, the *Midsummer Night's Dream*[5] Overture; these are the Beau Brummells of music.

I will say nothing about Chopin now except that my opinion is very like Schoenberg's, but Schubert is, I think, infinitely the richest of the composers you mention. As a student in St. Petersburg I knew his songs, piano music, quintets, quartets, trios, the last two symphonies, but little else. I was especially fond of the song cycles, though I considered that Schubert abused—was too ready to go to—the minor key, and that the strictly harmonic function of the piano and the resulting eternally arpeggiated piano accompaniments were monotonous.

Other young St. Petersburg musicians knew even less Schubert, which did not keep them from dismissing him as a 'peasant musi-

[5] The *Midsummer Night's Dream* incidental music ought to be used only for Schlegel's version of the play, the production of which should then be clothed in the provincial German court style of the period. No one can build a story ballet on a play whose substance is poetry and whose plot is only a peg. The most successful episode in Balanchine's ballet is the Divertimento danced to the String Symphony No. 9, but this is smuggled into the second act and has nothing to do with the story. Mendelssohn is banal only when he reaches for dramatic pathos, and when he does that he tends to anticipate Brahms—the passage in the *Melusine* that almost becomes a passage in Brahms' Second Symphony. I was disturbed, seeing Balanchine's ballet, by intemperate lengths in the *Dream* music. Even the flute *Scherzo* would be twice as magical if it were half as long. But that is the impression of an elderly and economical composer, of course, and Mendelssohn was a freely-spending young one.

cian' and, in one case, from asserting that Tchaikovsky had improved the theme of the 'Unfinished' Symphony in the theme song of *Swan Lake*. Few of my fellow students listened more deeply than that, though to compare the Schubert B minor symphony with *Swan Lake* is to learn, among many other things, that the Austrian peasant at least reassigns orchestral roles when he repeats and that he is never as square of phrase as my compatriot.

Schubert's most astonishing symphonic achievement, the Fourth Symphony, mocks the nonsense that the composer was unable to sustain large-scale developments but could only string together song forms. One cannot catalogue the *momenti lirici* of this masterpiece, but can only look at the musical whole. In the symphony, Schubert's feeling for the largest-extending tonality relationships, his harmonic skill, his powers of development, are to be compared only to those of Beethoven. And the symphony points to never-to-be-developed contrapuntal gifts, while at the same time it far surpasses the other composers you mention in the ripeness of its chromatic idiom—see measures 90–105, and the corresponding place, in the *Andante* movement; and compare the introduction with the introduction of Mozart's quartet in the same key; and look at measures 431–451, and the corresponding place, in the last movement; and the whole of the scherzo; and the change of key in the last movement, which, as timing, can be matched only by Beethoven; the chromatic idea is sustained through all four movements, too, and with a maturity that Mozart might have envied, at that precocious age of eighteen.

Schumann is a composer for whom I have a personal weakness,[6] but the symphony is not his domain. If I compare a symphony of his, say the D minor, which I have just heard, with the Schubert Fourth (admittedly an invidious comparison like all such), the Schumann seems not to be a symphony at all, in the Beethoven sense. It is naïve in construction and it was not conceived instrumentally, and these are a craftsman's remarks, as Gilbert Ryle would say, not public highway remarks. But, however far from Beethoven, the theme at measure 305 must have derived from the *Larghetto* in Beethoven's Second Symphony. The trio of the *Scherzo* is my favourite episode in the Fourth Symphony, but even there I

---

[6] I saw Clara Schumann, plain, in the summer of 1895 when my father took me as a translator—he did not speak German—to call upon her in a villa near Homburg-vor-der-Höhe. I remember a very old lady with a walking stick.

must say that I find the return of the trio much too punctual. And the first movement is altogether too rectangular (the trombone theme at measures 178, 182, 186, 190), and the *Romanza*, especially the embroidering violin triplets, is too faded even for dinner music in a Swiss hotel.

R.C.: And are you still enthusiastic about Gounod, Messager, and Lecocq? How do you compare Gounod and Bizet?

I.S.: Please, please. I had a certain taste for Lecocq at the time of *Mavra* and I wrote a *souvenir* of him into a flute melody in *Jeu de cartes*. He was a *musiquette* composer of gifts and originality. I own his autographed score of *Giroflé, Girofla*, and I still have a score of *La Coeur à la main*. Messager was less highly endowed, but he was a charming man, very kind and encouraging to me in my first years in Paris. He was to have conducted the first performance of *Le Rossignol*, but he backed out in favour of Monteux. As for Gounod, I was once greatly attracted by his melodic gifts, but I did not mean to condone his insipidity. Gounod blinded me to Bizet in my Russian years, and I could see nothing in the author of *Carmen* except an intelligent eclecticism. In the cold war of Tchaikovsky vs. Rimsky, *Carmen* was admired more by the Muscovite than by the Petersburg school. A case for plagiarism could be made against *Pique Dame*—compare Lisa's aria in the second act and the Lisa-Herman duet in the third act with *Carmen*'s card scene, and the Summer Garden chorus with the first scene in *Carmen*—but the plaintiff would have to admire Tchaikovsky's taste even as a thief. The card aria is the centrepiece of *Carmen* and, with the G-flat major smugglers' ensemble, the Quintet and José's last scene, its best music, a jewel, in fact, surrounded by semiprecious stones. The card aria is made with the simplest means, and embellished with a few masterful touches like the oboe and trombone octaves and the string appoggiaturas in the coda. I did not much admire *Carmen* until recent years. Micaëla bored me, and so did that absurd Flower Song, and all the *Prix de Rome* modulations. But these were period prejudices. *Carmen* was madly *démodé* by the time I became a composer. The vogue for the exotic, the foreign, the sham Spanish, was over, and the Broadway show-type opera—add a number, cut a number—in other words *Carmen*, was not yet *à la mode*. I considered it good cabaret music, but no more (which, indeed, some of it is: the '*Bel officier*' is pure Piaf, and Dancairo and Remendado in their duet '*Carmen, mon amour tu viendras*' are like two saxophones out of Guy Lombardo). The last *Carmen* I saw in Russia had some novel staging. A Red Cross ambulance was the only object in view at the end of the opera. It stood just outside the bull ring. The *metteur en scène* must have been an anti-Mithraist or a vegetarian.

With Pierre Boulez, Paris, May, 1962.

With Rex Harrison, New York, 1964.

PERSONAL

Contemporary Music and Recording

Con-tempo: 'with the times.' Con-tempo music is the most interesting music that ever has been written, and the present moment is the most exciting in music history. It always has been. Nearly all con-tempo music is bad, too, and so was it ever. The 'lament of present days,' as Byron called it, is as old as the first antiquarian.

Modern: *modernus, modo*: 'just now.' But, also, *modus*, 'manner,' whence 'up-to-date' and 'fashionable.' A more complex word, and evidently of urban origin, though I shall have to look this up in Latin and French poets. (*'Il faut être absolument moderne.'*)

And 'new music'? But surely that misplaces the emphasis. What is most new in new music dies quickest, and that which makes it live is all that is oldest and most tried. To contrast the new and the old is a *reductio ad absurdum*, and sectarian 'new music' is the blight of contemporaneity. Let us use con-tempo, then, not technically, in the sense that Schoenberg and Chaminade lived at the same time, but in my meaning: 'with the times.'

To the performer, a recording is valuable chiefly as a mirror. He is able to reflect himself in it, to walk away from his subjective experience and look at it. A recording session is a shuttling from subjective to objective, and the performer is like the muralist who has to back away from his work to see it in perspective. In my case the perspective of the object, the playback, dwindles to a point of identity when I conduct, and the located object, myself conducting the music, is replaced by, simply, the music—or, rather, as it is my music, myself in the music, for I am always aware of my being in my music. This mirroring is the main point, I think, and not whether a recording extends the range of peripheral hearing or canalizes hearing selectively (dangers as well as advantages): a record is a lever than can lift one outside of one's performance involvement, or 'far out' enough, at least, to establish the illusion.

Mirrors are also mnemonic devices. One sees what one was, rather than what one is; the immediate has too many shadings. One looks into one's mirrors and is aware only of the subtraction; one listens to oneself to compare. The point of view of another time is recognizable to me in other people's recordings of other composers, too, but my reaction to that is passive. But I imagine that any still-growing performer must be similarly disturbed.

By definition, contemporary music is unfamiliar, and, by deduction, it is more difficult than other types of music to record. (I do not say that it is more difficult to perform; it is and it isn't, in different ways.) The fifty recordings of the Beethoven symphony are fifty different angles of distortion, but these distortions actually protect the scope of the work: the larger the variorum, the greater the guarantee that Beethoven himself will remain intact. The recording of the contemporary, on the other hand, lacking comparison, fixes the music at a single angle, and the gravest danger of this fixed angle, which is that the truly contemporary exists on the precarious edge of the comprehensible, is not obvious. What is wrong with the Beethoven performance is evident and cannot damage the work, but what is wrong in the performance of the unfamiliar work is not always evident, and the line between sense and nonsense in it may, and often does, depend upon its performance. The difference between a Kandinsky and a doodler, a Schoenberg and a lunatic, was apparent to only a few imaginative and highly trained perceivers in 1912. We know that even such a close disciple as Alban Berg could not at that time readily follow *Pierrot lunaire*. It is axiomatic, then, that performances of the unfamiliar are a greater responsibility and must seek higher standards than performance of the familiar. Every first recording is a risk.

The question of value in repertory versus non-repertory: I see no artistic reason to proliferate recordings of music that is widely performed live. I mean the concertos in B flat minor, the tone poems in E flat major, the symphonies in E minor. A recording is, or should be, a performance, and who can suffer exactly the same set of performance limitations more than once—at least with familiar music? I do suffer them when the music is unfamiliar, but with less pain because they do not distract unduly from the learning process, the becoming familiar. The recording of non-repertory, of what is not generally available live, should be the *raison d'être* of the industry. How many people in the United States have heard live performances of Schoenberg's larger dramatic works? The answer —in full figures for per capita comparison—is 000,000,000, and the conclusion is obvious: recordings, rather than isolated and sporadic concerts, are the chief means of communication between the contemporary composer and his audience.

A footnote on non-repertory with another meaning of that term: non-existent. An advertisement for a new disc from the current catalogue says something about 'Stokowski's Bach.' But no such Bach ever existed. 'Bach's Stokowski' would make more sense historically. And I have just received an album with a blurb about 'The great conductor' von K.'s 'Mozart.' But what does von K.'s conducting really do to Mozart? It opens his bier, unclasps his hands from his bosom, and folds them behind his head.

I have just received some programmes of a concert series in Leningrad dedicated to my later music. Every musician—composer, conductor, music educator—to whom I have shown them has pronounced the same comment: 'I wonder what the performances sounded like, as no one there has heard the music.' In other words, the printed page is no longer regarded as self-sufficient, but is expected, as a matter of course, to be supplemented by a recorded guide.

What are my attitudes to my own recorded performances? I have already said that I only listen to them critically and that I could not do any of them the same way again. But even the poorest are valid readings to guide other performers, and the best, like the new *Zvezdoliki*, is very good indeed. What are the poorest? Those pieces which were too new to me, and for which I had no settled ideas and technical habits of performance. The first recordings of *The Rake's Progress*, *Lulu*, and *Moses und Aron* have very effectively helped to kill those operas in America, where they were known for a long time only by records.

What, to a composer, is most important about a recorded performance? The spirit, of course, the same as in any performance and the spirit of some recent recordings of my music has fallen arches. Next to the spirit come the two chief questions of the flesh: tempo and balance. I am annoyed by the violin solo in my *Agon* recording. It seems to emanate from the bedroom, while the trombone accompaniment sounds as though it is in my lap. But imbalances of this sort were common in early stereo recordings, and whereas a monaural was a closet, an early stereo was three closets. We also heard things we had never heard before. but we didn't always want to. Now we have learned to let backgrounds be backgrounds, like bygones, and we know that acoustics pretends to be, but is not yet, a science. Still I am even more irritated by an impossible tempo. If the speeds of everything in the world and in ourselves have changed, our tempo feelings cannot remain unaffected. The metronome marks one wrote forty years ago were contemporary forty years ago. Time is not alone in affecting tempo—circumstances do too, and every performance is a different equation of them. I would be surprised if any of my own recent recordings follows the metronome markings.

'Live music is at least a performance'—which is meant to imply that recordings are not. In fact, though, performers can be inspired even in recording studios and the concentration there is at least as great as it is in concerts. With technically complex contemporary music, true performance on records, though it should always be the goal, is difficult to attain. The published version is usually a pastiche of excerpts from the best of several forays. I can make this clear only by a description of such a session.

It lasts three hours. The music has not been rehearsed and the first two hours are therefore used in spot-rehearsing it. During this time, microphones are adjusted, balance tests are made, positions of instruments are changed, and sometimes the whole orchestra is reseated. The conductor's faculties are entirely concentrated on the problem of when to stop and explain or correct—on deciding what a player or an orchestra is likely to resolve the next time around on its own and what it will never understand without prompting and explanation. This is a matter of the conductor's and the orchestra's experience, but not entirely of that, and some part of the decision will always be a gamble. When this perfunctory contact with the music is over and the actual recording has begun, the attention of the conductor is turned to the clock. From then on he becomes a machine for making decisions. Can this section be improved if it is played once more, and how much time remains, and how much music has still to be recorded? The recording director will advise him to go on, of course, telling him that the section may be repeated 'if time is left at the end' (quotation from the standard A-&-R recording director's manual), but every recording session is a photo finish, and even if one could return to something recorded earlier, the sound levels would not match.

Editing and preparing the master record from such a session is an equally interesting non-musical exercise, largely because the morticians who cut tape have developed a delightful vocabulary: scrub the tuba, dig for the cellos, echo the splice, goose the singer at 500 and dip her at 3,000. But if I were to expose the realities of editing, I would bury the bluff about performance and kill the sale of records.

If the conductor is the surgeon in this three-hour operation, his anaesthetist is the A-&-R supervisor. This accomplice must be a virtuoso listener and score-reader, a child psychologist, and a liar ('Marvellous take, everybody'). He also must know his artist to such an extent that he can keep him directed toward a performance that the artist himself may have lost sight of. And he must hide his boredom, too, for he spends most of his time recording the Liberaces of classical music, and the contemporary music he does do (in this case not contemporary, but modern) is likely to be the gimmicky pieces for vibraphones, *Sprechstimme*, and *ponticello*—in other words, sound effects rather than music.

Thoughts of an Octogenarian

'And in his old age the wisdom of his song shall exceed even the beauties of his youth; and it shall be much loved' (Psellus Akritas of Alexandria, *De Ceremoniis*, XIV, 7).

I was born out of time in the sense that by temperament and talent I would have been more suited for the life of a small Bach, living in anonymity and composing regularly for an established service and for God. I did weather the world I was born to, weathered it well, you might say, and I have survived—though not uncorrupted—

the hucksterism of publishers, music festivals, recording companies, publicity—including my own ('Self-love is unquestionably the chief motive which leads anyone to speak, and more especially to write, respecting himself,' Alfieri, *Memoirs*)—conductors, critics (with whom my real argument is that the person who practises the vocation of music should not be judged by the person who has no vocation and does not understand musical practice, and to whom music must therefore be of infinitely less fundamental consequence), and all of the misunderstandings about performance the word concerts has come to mean. But the small Bach might have composed three times as much music.

At eighty I have found new joy in Beethoven, and the Great Fugue now seems to me—it was not always so—a perfect miracle. How right Beethoven's friends were when they convinced him to detach it from Opus 130, for it must stand by itself, this absolutely contemporary piece of music that will be contemporary for ever. (I wonder, do these statements surprise students of my own later work, the Great Fugue being all variation and development whereas my later music is all canonic and therefore static and objective—in fact, the antithesis of Beethoven's fugue? Do students of my music expect me to cite something like Josquin's *Hic me sidereo* as my 'favourite' piece?) Hardly birthmarked by its age, the Great Fugue is as rhythm alone more subtle than any music composed in my own century. What, for example, are the consequences implied by the notation? It is pure interval music, this fugue, and I love it beyond any other.

An example of a musical antithesis to me in my own time is *Wozzeck*. What disturbs me about this great masterpiece and one that I love, is the level of its appeal to 'ignorant' audiences, with whom one may attribute its success to: (1) the story; (2) Bible, child sentiment; (3) sex; (4) brevity; (5) dynamics, pppp to ffff^n; (6) muted brass, ∧, ▼, *col legno*, etc.; (7) the idea that the vocal line ∿ = emotion; (8) the orchestral flagellation in the interludes; (9) the audience's feeling that it is being modern.

'Passionate emotion' can be conveyed by very different means than these, and within the most 'limiting conventions.' The Timurid miniaturists, for example, were forbidden to portray facial expression. In one moving scene, from the life of an early Zoroastrian king, the artist shows a group of totally blank faces. The dramatic tension is in the way the ladies of the court are shown eavesdropping, and in the slightly discordant gesture of one of the principal figures. In another of these miniatures, two lovers confront each other with stony looks, but the man unconsciously touches his finger to his lips, and this packs the picture with, for me, as much passion as the *crescendo molto* in *Wozzeck*.

The dualism of the self and the containing body widens, as though I had become the demonstration instrument in a Platonic form-argument; and the container is more foreign each day, and more of a penance. I wish to walk faster, but my unwilling partner will not execute the wish, and one imminent tomorrow it will refuse to move at all, at which time I shall insist upon an even sharper distinction between the alien form instrument and myself. At four-score, the alienation of the body-image is a necessary psychological safety device, and those Swiss Lourdes's of glandular and cellular rejuvenation are indispensable articles of belief.

The brain cells are unique in that they cannot be renewed. May I adduce from this that we are born with our talents, that we may 'think' or 'will' ourselves into command of them, but that the thinking and willing potentiality is given, that I was born with the possibility of becoming a composer, and the circumstances of my formation have made me this composer?

I regard my talents as God-given, and I have always prayed to Him for strength to use them. When in early childhood I discovered that I had been made the custodian of musical aptitudes, I pledged myself to God to be worthy of their development, though, of course, I have broken the pledge and received uncovenanted mercies all my life, and though the custodian has too often kept faith on his own all-too-worldly terms.

Creation is its own image and thought is its own mirror. As I think about this metaphor language—it gives me claustrophobia—the word mirror frightens me. Seventy-five years ago as a child alone in my room, I once saw my father instead of myself in the looking glass, and my already strong case of father-fears became mirror-fears as well. I expect Purgatory to be lined with many-dimensional mirrors.

What about the 'infinity of possibilities' in connection with the new art material of electronically produced sound? With few exceptions 'infinite possibilities' has meant collages of organ burbling, rubber suction noises, machine-gunning, and other —this is curious—representational and associative noises more appropriate to Mr. Disney's musical mimicries. Not the fact of possibilities, of course, but choice is the beginning of art. But the sound lab. is already a part of the musical supermarket. (Especially in the field of publicity. The structure of a new piece by Xenakis is advertised as having been 'worked out on the IBM 7090 electronic computer' as if that were a guarantee of quality.) I know of a composer who wanted 'something electronic, kind of middle range, bassoon-trombone like'—these were his only instructions to the sound engineer, who nevertheless flipped a toggle switch, made a few connections, and handed the composer an envelope containing a tape of the desired noise. The composition, I am told, sounds like 'electronic Brahms.'

Sounds by themselves may be aesthetic, or, at least, painful or pleasurable, but to me they are only a putative material of music. They have another use, too, and a fascinating one, in the field of audio-analgesics. But a composer is not, by intention, a musical therapist.

An electronic machine cannot dehumanize (whatever that may be); indeed, it can only do what it has been directed to do. It may extend memory functions, for example, when a man has established its memory locations and devised the means to signal and connect them. But the most nearly perfect musical machine, a Stradivarius or an electronic synthesizer, is useless until joined to a man with musical skill and imagination. The stained-glass artists of Chartres had few colours, and the stained-glass artists of today have hundreds of colours but no Chartres. Organs, too, have more stops now than ever before, but no Bach. Not enlarged resources, then, but men and what they believe.

What is the 'human measure' in music? And is this a possible question? Isn't the wish to prescribe merely another intance of the fear of becoming other, of changing the past? And, in any case, won't the 'human measure' *be* whatever we agree it ought to be? As for myself, I am no more concerned with a definition Man than I am with subjective grunts like 'good' and 'bad.' My 'human measure' is not only possible, but also exact. It is, first of all, absolutely physical, and it is immediate. I am made bodily ill, for example, by sounds electronically spayed for overtone removal. To me they are a castration threat.

Time, too, is a physical measure to me, and in music I must feel a physical here and there and not only a now, which is to say, movement from and toward. I do not always feel this sense of movement or location in, say, Boulez's *Structures* or those fascinating score-plans by Stockhausen (I have not yet heard his *Momente* for voices and thirteen instruments, but the title augurs well), and though every element in those pieces may be organized to engender motion, the result often seems to me like the essence of the static. A time series may very well postulate a new parable about time, but that is not the same thing as a time experience, which for me is dynamic passage through time. Nor, of course, are these composers concerned about 'dynamic passage through,' which betrays an essentially dramatic concept, Greek in origin, like all of my ideas of musical form. The very phrase exposes the gulf between myself and the Teddy Boys of music, and between me and the Zen generation as a whole, and so does their favourite word, vector, which for me is a metaphor in no way analogous to a musical experience, vector being a spatial concept to me, and music a temporal art.

Anyone who survives a sixty-year span of creative activity in our century must sometimes feel a satisfaction merely in being able to metabolize new experience, to 'stay with it'; or, any rate, this appears to be a greater feat now, where the 'ins' are in for a shorter term than in the time of such octogenarians (so far as one can judge other times and generalize about octogenarians) as Sophocles, Voltaire, and Goethe, and where no one can be *primus inter pares*, or hold not only the historical centre but even the redoubts for more than two or three years.

I was born to causality and determinism, and I have survived to probability theory and chance. I was born to a world that explained itself largely in dogmatic terms and I have lived, through several changes of management, to a world that rationalizes itself almost entirely in psychoanalytic terms. Educated by simple fact—the trigger one squeezed was what shot the gun—I have had to learn that, in fact, the universe of anterior contributing possibilities was responsible. But I was also born to a non-progressivist notion of the practice of my art, and on this point, though I have survived into a musical society that pursues the opposite idea, I have not been able to change. I do not understand the composer who says we must analyse and determine the evolutionary tendency of the whole musical situation and proceed from there. I have never consciously analysed any musical situation, and I can follow only where my musical appetites lead me.

And how are we to know 'the whole musical situation'? I am something of an aldermanic figure in music today and a composer still considered to be capable of development in some departments of musical practice, yet recently, trying to read an essay on current techniques by a foremost scholiast of supraserial music, I discovered that I understood hardly a word—or, rather, hardly a diagram, for the essay looked like an IBM punch card. Whether I am a forefront or rear-guard or road-hog composer is beside the point, which is the disparity between the doer and the explainer. As a doer I have not been able to 'keep up' even in my own specialized and ever-narrowing preserves. And because anything one writes is already out of date on publication (re-read the first page of these pensées and you will see that it has become quite mouldy), the professional literature of the future (which is now) can consist only of summaries and supplements—developments in the field during the previous week. Dr. Toynbee's last book was called 'Volume Twelve: Reconsiderations.' And Volume Thirteen? Further Reconsiderations? And so on.

'Mortify the past.' The past as a wish that creates the probability pattern of the future? Did John of the Cross mean that, and the fear of changing the past which is fear of the present? I mortify *my* past every time I sit at the piano to compose, in any case, though I have no wish to go back or to relive a day of my life. But I have relived much in recent years. Four cerebral thromboses seem to have unshuttered the remotest reaches of memory or spilled a restorative chemical over the palimpsest of my baby book. I have been able to roam in the park of my childhood as I could not a decade ago, but I tug at my memory only as a mountain-climber tugs at his rope: to see how and where it is tied; I do not go back, in the threat of time, because of a wish to return. And even though my subconscious may be trying to close the circle, I want to go on rectilinearly as always: the dualism again. The archaeologist's dream—Renan's—of the whole past recaptured is another of my visions of Purgatory, and the poet's dream—Coleridge's—of restoring the collective experience of a mind's whole past existence is, to me, an insanity threat.

My agenbite of inwit is that I do not know while composing, am not aware of, the value question. I love whatever I am now doing, and with each new work I feel that I have at last found the way, have just begun to compose. I love all of my children, of course, and, like any father, I am inclined to favour the backward and imperfectly formed ones. But I am actually excited only by the newest (Don Juanism?) and the youngest (nymphetism?). I hope, too, that my best work is still to be written (I want to write a string quartet and a symphony), but 'best' means nothing to me while I am composing, and comparisons of the sort that other people make about my music are to me invidious or simply absurd.

Was I merely trying to refit old ships while the other side—Schoenberg—sought new forms of travel? I believe that this distinction, much traded on a generation ago, has disappeared. (An era is shaped only by hindsight, of course, and hindsight reduces to convenient unities, but all artists know that they are part of the same thing.) Of course I seemed to have exploited an apparent discontinuity, to have made art out of the *disjecta membra*, the quotations from other composers, the references to earlier styles ('hints of earlier and other creation'), the detritus that betokened a wreck. But I used it, and anything that came to hand, to rebuild, and I did not pretend to have invented new conveyors or new means of travel. But the true business of the artist *is* to refit old ships. He can say again, in his way, only what has already been said.

APPENDIX A

Menzies Hotel
Melbourne
November 27, 1961

Editor
The Observer
22 Tudor Street
London

Sir:

Peter Heyworth's *Schnabel the Creator* (*The Observer*, November 10, 1961) quotes a remark by Glazunov printed in a book of Schnabel's writings I have not read: 'Of all the 2,000 pupils I taught at the Conservatory in St. Petersburg, Stravinsky had the worst ear.' I was never Glazunov's pupil, never a student in the St. Petersburg Conservatory, and Glazunov's only opportunity to judge my ear was through my music, a test *he* failed.

Glazunov was almost as much of an idol to me in my fifteenth year as Rimsky himself, until I transcribed one of his string quartets for piano and impulsively took the score to his house to show it to him. Though I had never been presented to him, he knew my father, but in spite of which he received me ungraciously, perfunctorily flipping through my manuscript and pronouncing my work unmusical. I went away thoroughly discouraged. Now, though his later dislike was clearly due to the fact that I had not come to him for instruction but had gone directly to Rimsky, I cannot explain this early incident. As for Rimsky's own opinion of Glazunov, I can say only that the success of any pupil made him proud, and Glazunov was his most apparent success. To an academically minded man like Rimsky, Glazunov must also have seemed the safest of the younger composers, in the sense that the only rule he could ever undermine would be the rule of imagination.

A short time later, when I began to wonder at myself for having been interested in Glazunov in the past (the whiteness pilled from my eyes, as the translator of Tobit says), I continued to see him at Conservatory concerts, often in company with that other reckless academician, Tcherepnin. He was always rude to me but I think that was because my remark that he was only a Carl Philipp Emanuel Rimsky-Korsakov had been repeated to him. After the first performance of my Symphony in E flat he told me that he thought it 'rather heavy instrumentation for such empty music.' He was also present at the performance of my instrumentations of Beethoven's and Mussorgsky's 'Flea' songs for a Goethe-in-music concert conducted by Siloti, and at the première of my *Fireworks*. This time his comment was repeated to me: '*Kein talent, nur Dissonanz.*'

I have told elsewhere how in 1935 Maria Kuznetzov's son came to my studio in the Salle Pleyel and begged me to greet my 'old St. Petersburg colleague' during intermission of a rehearsal of his music downstairs. I accompanied Kuznetzov to Glazunov's green room, but was greeted with as little sympathy—he extended two fingers and said nothing—as I had received thirty-eight years before.

All this has nothing to do with Schnabel, of course, except to say that our experiences of Glazunov were different. (Schnabel found him charming.) My encounters with Schnabel in Berlin in the 1920's and in New York during the 1939 war were pleasant enough, and I always had the greatest respect for Schnabel as a pedagogue. (I even tried to persuade him to take my younger son as a pupil.) But my encounters with his music were another matter. All the examples I have met with were timeless in the wrong sense (Schoenberg is reported to have told him that 'rests are also permitted in twelve-tone music'), and one of them, a solo cello sonata, was probably the unloveliest lucubration I have ever heard. To me, 'Schnabel the Creator' is a tenuous proposition and in the old word-association game, his masterpiece, the *Duodecimet*, would only make me say 'ulcers.'

Yours, etc.
IGOR STRAVINSKY

APPENDIX B

Soon after the publication of V. Yastrebtzev's *Recollections of Rimsky-Korsakov* Volume II (Moscow, 1962), scholars began to ask me for comment on the book's references to myself. I remember nothing about Yastrebtzev beyond the name, however, and when I try to associate that with my memory of faces in Rimsky's group, I confuse it with the librettist Belsky. The book is an accurate picture of Rimsky and his circle, though, and I am certain that it is a reliable chronicle.

Yastrebtzev first mentions me under the date February 28, 1903, merely identifying me as a young musician. Most of the other fifty-three references to me occur in memos of conversations at Rimsky's weekly gatherings, the *jours fixes* at which compositions by his pupils were performed and discussed.

Yastrebtzev notes that on March 6, 1903, I played my *plaisanteries musicales* at Rimsky's, but I have no recollection of these bagatelles. On February 17, 1904, he writes that I played my *chanson comique* and that Nicolas Richter horrified Rimsky's wife by playing a cakewalk. He adds that 'Mitussov and Stravinsky amusingly demonstrated how it should be danced.' Paws up, like circus poodles, or boop-boop-a-doop?

The entry of March 6, 1904, states that 'During dinner the young Rimsky-Korsakovs, with Stravinsky at their head, performed a charming cantata which Stravinsky had composed and dedicated to Nicolai Andreitch. The cantata was repeated by audience request.' I have no recollection of this *Tafelmusik*.

The notes for August 22 and 23, 1904, written at Vehchasha, near Lzy,[1] state that Rimsky was 'forcing' me to work in the orchestration, for winds, of the Polonaise from *Pan Voyevoda*.

---

[1] See *Expositions and Developments*, p. 35.

APPENDIX B

I quote Yastrebtzev directly for a few other entries that may be of interest:

February 9, 1905. Before tea, N. Richter played the F sharp minor sonata, dedicated to him, by Stravinsky.

March 6, 1906. At the beginning of the musical progamme, Igor Stravinsky played his *Conductor in Tarantula.* [I think this was a piano piece inspired by *Koosma Prootkov.*—I.S.][2]

February 27, 1907. Stravinsky's romances were sung.

April 18, 1907. Among those present was I. F. Stravinsky, to whom Nicolai Andreitch presented the orchestra score of the *Tableau of Tsar Saltan.* [Rimsky gave me this manuscript to commemorate the first performance of my Symphony in E flat.—I.S.]

October 31, 1907. After tea, Stravinsky and Steinberg played Stravinsky's *Pastorale* twice, singing on the vowel A. Stravinsky then presented his *Novice*, on the three first words—the bell sounds —of Gorodetsky's poem. The middle of the piece is beautiful, but the beginning is strange. Is it music or is it 'on purpose'?

November 4, 1907. In the opinion of Rimsky-Korsakov, the talent of Igor Stravinsky has not yet taken clear shape. Rimsky thinks that the fourth part of his Symphony imitates Glazunov too much, and Rimsky himself. And he considers that in the new romances on words of Gorodetsky, Igor Feodorovitch puts himself too much on the side of *modernism.*

December 25, 1907. After the performance of Stravinsky's *Pastorale* and *Spring*, Rimsky said: 'I hold to my opinion of the *Spring*. What pleasure can anyone have in composing music to the words of such false Russian folk language? For me, all this "lyrical impressionism" is contemporary decadence. It is full of mist and fog, but meagre in content of ideas.'

January 15, 1908. Talk about the Symphony by Igor Stravinsky. The orchestration of the first part is too heavy, but there are handsome harmonic and instrumental episodes. The Symphony will be performed by the Court Orchestra on the 22nd January—Tuesday. [Gossip after a rehearsal, evidently.—I.S.]

February 16, 1908. Everyone was at the Belaiev concert yesterday, conducted by F. Blumenfeld. Stravinsky's Suite *Le Faune et la bergère.*

---

[2] See *Memories and Commentaries*, p. 142.

LETTERS ON 'OEDIPUS REX'

Mr. Jean Cocteau
a Villefranche s/M

Mon cher Jean,
L'idée qui me poursuit depuis un certain temps de composer un opéra en langue latine sur un sujet d'une tragédie du monde antique que chacun connaiterait je voudrais t'en confier la réalisation verbale comme je te l'ai proposé l'autre jour. Le scénarium ainsi que la mis-en-scène seraient réalisé par notre intime collaboration.

Je t'écris ces lignes poussé par le besoin du plus de clarté possible dans tout ce qui résulte d'une pareille collaboration.

Laissant de côté dans cette lettre les questions de répartition des droits d'auteurs, d'édition etc, qui feront l'objet d'une convention spéciale entre nous, je voudrais que ces lignes fussent le témoignage de la promesse que nous nous sommes mutuellement donné de garder le secret de notre collaboration non seulement tant que celle-ci durera, mais même quand la pièce sera achevée, c.à.d. ne jamais en parler sous quelque forme que ce soit (livres, lettres, articles, interview, discours).

Dans le cas peu probable, je l'éspère, où nous ne tomberions pas d'accord sur la question 'affaire' (droits d'auteurs, éditeurs etc.) dont j'ai parlé plus haut et que cette collaboration n'aurait pas lieu, je me reserve le droit de réaliser sous n'importe quelle forme mon idée, que je garde jalousement, d'une pièce musicale avec texte latin.

Nice le 11 oct 1925

Je t'embrasse
I. STR.

L'original de cette lettre où figure sous ma signature la signature de Cocteau avec 'lu et approuvé' doit probablement se trouver chez 'l'Ed. Russe de Musique' avec le contrat de Cocteau et autre pièces regardant le côté 'affaire' de notre collaboration.

I. STR.
Voreppe 4.II.32

LETTERS ON 'OEDIPUS REX'

A draft by Cocteau (with transcription) for the Speaker's last narration in *Oedipus Rex*, with fanfares added by Stravinsky. The text (except for the second paragraph) is close to that of the completed work.

Tromp. Et maintenant, vous allez entendre le monologue illustre 'La tête divine de Jocaste est morte', monologue où le messager raconte la fin de Jocaste. *Tromp.* Il peut à peine ouvrir la bouche. Le choeur emprunte son rôle et l'aide a dire comment la reine s'est pendue et comment Oedipe s'est crevé les yeux, avec son agrafe d'or. (*Tromp.*)
Et soudain apparait la chose atroce: Le piège d'Oedipe. Le piège a fonctionné. Oedipe était le piège d'Oedipe. Oedipe renferme Oedipe. Oedipe est seul dans la nuit d'Oedipe. Les dieux se désintéressent. Le roi est pris.

Ensuite, c'est l'épilogue. Epilogue: Le roi est pris. Il veut se montrer dans son piège. Il veut se montrer à tous, montrer à tous la bête immonde, l'inceste, le parricide, le fou. On le chasse. On le chasse avec une extrême douceur. Adieu, adieu, pauvre Oedipe. Adieu Oedipe; on t'aimait. *Tromp.*

Villefranche
Mars 1926

Mon cher Jean,
 Je suis stupéfait de la conduite de Diaghilew. Quand-même, quelle indiscretion! Il tâche à tout prix de dévoiler la surprise que je lui avais promis, chose incroyable cette attitude qu'il prend devant un hommage (et non une affaire!!!! qu'il le sache bien) qu'on est en train de lui préparer. Je te prie de lui dire exactement ce que je viens de t'écrire.
 En t'interrogeant à propos du sujet même de l'oeuvre il a l'air de savoir que c'est précisement avec toi que je collabore. A moins que ça soit une pure provocation et j'espère tu ne t'y es pas laissé prendre. Dis lui aussi qu'il ferait bien mieu de répondre aux lettres qu'on lui écrit au lieu de tâcher de dévoiler la surprise derière mon dos. Je lui ai écris à Montecarlo et n'ai reçu aucune réponse—
 Quand à toi-même, Jean, je m'étonne que tu pose la question du silence. Mais bien entendu, parbleu! N'en éprouve-tu pas toi-même le besoin?
 En ce moment-même je reçois ton cable. Je te télégraphie; donc tout s'arrange très bien. J'avais besoin de te voir pour règler certaines questions d'organisation générale (Comité, Polignac etc.) ainsi que pour différants détails d'édition (je viens de recevoir l'épreuve du Ier acte)— texte latin, speaker etc.
 Fait tranquillement tes picures et retablis-toi vite. Catherine va de mieu en mieu et t'envoie ses bonnes amitiés.

             Je t'embrasse
             ton I. STRAWINSKY

Nice, le 10 févr., 27

Prince A. Zeretelli
Paris

Cher Prince,

Merci de votre lettre du 17 cr.—En principe j'accepte, mais de faite, comme je vous l'ai dit dans ma dernière lettre il faut que vous vous adressiez a Mr. André Aron, car c'est lui qui est chargé d'examiner les contrats et de faire les payements necessaires.

Je vois d'après les prix qui s'établissent que les chanteurs-solistes plus les choeurs nous reviendrons en chiffre rond à 20 mille fr. Il ne faut pas que cela dépasse.

Je vous prie donc de voir au plus vite Mr. Aron en lui disant qu'avec les prix que vous me donnez je suis d'accord et que s'il a déjà les sommes indispensables on peut établir les contrats et les signer.

En attendant de vos bonnes nouvelles, je vous envoie; cher Prince, mes meilleures amitiés.

I. STRAWINSKY

Nice, le 19/III/27

Jean Cocteau
Paris

Mon cher Jean,

Je viens de t'envoyer un cable d'ou tu peux voir que la chose ne se décidant toujours pas j'ai du abandonner Oedipe à sa propre vie c.à.d. que n'importe qui voulant le jouer n'a qu'à s'adresser à mon éditeur qui est le propriétaire de la pièce.

La première étant depuis longtemps promise à Diaghilew qui arrangeait son programme d'après cette promesse il me fallait lui demander s'il tenait de le jouer lui avant les autres. Il m'a répondu que s'était avec joie qu'il le ferait. Il prendra les décors de Théodore et réalisera la pièce telle qu'elle était concue. Quand à moi, j'ai renoncé à diriger Oedipe ne voulant en aucune sorte allourdir le budjet de l'affaire. Diaghilew invitera les éxécutants (chef d'orch., chanteurs, speaker, choeur etc.) qu'il voudra; exactement comme l'aurait fait tout autre théâtre. Mon rôle se bornera aux indications habituelles que j'ai coutume de donner quand on joue une oeuvre de moi. Voila le contrerendu officiel de l'affaire.

Et ce qui n'est pas de l'ordre officiel c'est que j'ai vu clair qu'il m'était impossible de m'occuper de la réalisation très compliquée quand à trouver des sommes necessaires, engagements des artistes etc. pendant mon travail très urgent de l'instrumentation. D'autre part il m'était trop pénible et je ne te le cache pas de voir s'accumuler autour de cette affaire rien que des potins (aulieu de l'entousiasme) qui me touche moi particulièrement de près.

Quand à Chanel qui voulait me voir comme tu me l'écrivait 'le plus vite possible' me répond à mon cable seulement vendredi dernier en me disant qu'elle allait en Espagne, qu'elle reviendrait probablement dans 10 jours à Paris et qu'elle me prie de lui écrire làbas. Donc tu l'a mal compris et elle n'était nullement pressée de prendre des décisions qui étaient de toute urgence pour nous. A vrai dire je n'ai autre chose à lui écrire maintenant que de la remercier d'avoir bien voulu s'interesser à la réalisation d'Oedipe mais que vu le temps très pressé pour prendre les décisions j'ai du renoncer à m'en occuper et j'ai remis l'affaire à Diaghilew.

Et en ce qui concerne Mme de Polignac je lui écrirai en la remerciant d'avoir offert des fonds pour la réalisation d'Oedipe en lui disant que je renonce de le diriger et que je la prie de remettre ces fonds à Diaghikew qui ne comptant pas de monter Oedipe lui même manquerait certainement des moyens necessaires.

Merci mille fois pour l'exposition de Théodore qui en est tout ce qu'il ya de plus heureux.

A bientot je t'embrasse
STRAWIGOR

Nice, le 11 avr./27

DIAGHILEW HOTEL DE PARIS MONTECARLO
COCTEAU ECRIT QUE CHANEL RENTREE VOYAGE OFFRE
SOMMES NECESSAIRES AUSSI BIEN A TOI SI VOUDRAIT
MONTER OEDIPESSTOP REPOND PAR NOUVEL TON AVIS
EMBRASSE STRAWIGOR
Strawinsky 167 Brd Carnot Nice

Prince Zeretelli
Paris

Mon cher Prince,

J'ai reçu votre lettre du 15 cr. Diaghilew me dit en même temps qu'il vous a télégraphié pourque vous engagiez chanteurs et choeur. Il s'agit maintenant d'éxécuter Oedipe en forme de concert, changement survenu assez subitement vu que ni moi ni Diaghilew ne possédons pas le temps nécessaire pour monter cette oeuvre importante en forme théatrale. Ayant trouvé les fonds nécessaires pour ces trois représentations d'Oedipe en forme de concert (qui passeront dans ses spectacles) j'ai remis à Diaghilew tous les soins de l'affaire. Donc pour vous rien n'est changé sinon qu'au lieu de s'adresser à moi pour tout ce qui concerne cette affaire il vous faudra vous adresser uniquement à Diaghilew.

En ce qui conserne votre proposition de Riga je veux bien consacrer une semaine, dix jours tout au plus le voyage y compris. Mes conditions pour ces deux concerts seraient $500 par concert plus frais chemin de fer et visa passeport. Comme date je préfère le commencement d'automne et le prix que je vous fixe ici doit être net c.a.d. exempt de toute commission, impôts etc. qui est à la charge de l'entreprise, comme la location du matériel musical procurable chez mes éditeurs dont je ne me charge absolument pas.

Quant à la Russie je ne crois pas que je puisse y aller cette année ayant entrepris trop de choses pour la saison prochaine.

A bientôt, cher Prince, je serai à Paris commencement mai.

Votre bien sincèrement dévoué

IGOR STRAWINSKY

Nice, le 17/IV/27.

Prince A. Zeretelli
Paris

Cher Prince,
votre bonne lettre du 26 cr. Reçu et vous en remercie.

Je serai à Paris le commencement de la semaine prochaine et nous causeron de Riga tranquillement.

Quant à la question de changement de conditions des solistes vu que s'est Diaghilew qui s'occupe de l'exécution d'Oedipe il y a un malentendu complet. Il faut que les artistes comprennent que s'est toujours moi qui me suis occupé de trouver des fonds necessaires pour cette exécution et le rôle de Diaghilew la-dedans est simplement un coup de main d'ami pour m'enlever toutes les peines d'une organisation qui me prendrait beaucout de temps et de forces au moment ou je travaille à l'achèvement de la part. d'orchestre. Expliquer leur mon cher Prince bien cela et assurer les qu'il n'y a aucun trucage la dedans ni de ma part ni de la part de Diaghilew.

Diagh. vient ces jours-ci à Paris, Nouvel y vient d'arriver et vous tranquillisera au point de vue matériel pour le choeur et les artistes. Je fais avec mon editeur tout pour établir ce matériel au plus vite. Ayez encore un peu de patience et soyez assuré que c'est aussi dans mon intérêt de voir tout le monde à l'étude de mon oeuvre à temps voulu.

A ces jours-ci, mon cher Prince, et en vous remerciant beaucoup de vos bonnes salutations je vous envoie toutes mes meilleures amitiés.

Votre IGOR STRAWINSKY

Nice, le 28/IV/27

Cher Jean

tu fais erreur si tu pense que je te demandais pardon dans ma dernière lettre me sentant en quelque sorte fautif devant toi en ce qui concerne Oedipe. Je n'ai absolument rien à me reprocher envers toi à cet égard et te demandais pardon simplement allant en ce moment à la Communion comme je te l'écrivais.

Quant à ta phrase que 'ennuieuse est la victoire de Serge qui ne voulait à aucun prix les décors de Théodore' elle ne saurait être qu'une supposition de ta part car au contraire Diagh. a passé toute la soirée avec Théodore en examinant ses décors, en les trouvant très bien et en lui donnant quelques conseils en vue de la prochaine exécution. Il a également trouvé que c'était bien le temps pour Théodore de faire une exposition et Théodore lui a montré les pièces qu'il avait l'intention d'exposer et entre autre les maquettes d'Oedipe.

A bientôt, je viens la semaine prochaine à Paris

je t'embrasse

I. STRAWINSKY

P.S.

Reçu la lettre de Walter des 4 chemins, je te prie de lui téléphonner mes remerciements et de lui dire que Théodore lui écrit lui-même.

Nice; le 28/IV/27

INDEX OF WORKS BY STRAVINSKY

Indexes compiled by Roger Savage

Abraham and Isaac, 45, 108
Agon, 54, 62, 122
Apollo, 18, 32–36, 48

Babel (*Genesis Suite*), 106
Le Baiser de la fée, 27

Cantata (1904), 133
Cantata (1952), 74
Capriccio, 54, 105, 115
Chanson comique, 133
Circus Polka, 52–53
Concerto for Piano and Wind Instruments, 108
Concerto for Two Pianos, 40, 42–43
Concerto for Violin and Orchestra, 42, 47–48
Concerto in D for Strings (*Basiliensis*), 148
Concerto in E flat ('Dumbarton Oaks'), 102
Conductor in Tarantula, 134

Danses concertantes, 34
Dialogue between Reason and Joy (unfinished, used in *Perséphone*), 38
Duo Concertant, 42

Easy Pieces for Piano Duet, 40–42
Ebony Concerto, 52–53
Eight Instrumental Miniatures, 112

The Fairy's Kiss, see *Le Baiser de la fée*
Le Faune et la bergère, 134

The Firebird, 34, 97, 108, 110
Fireworks, 132
The Flood, 24, 45, 57, 72–80, 110

Histoire du soldat, 39, 54, 106

Jeu de cartes, 117

Little Suites for Orchestra, see Easy Pieces

Mavra, 117
Movements, 62

The Nightingale, 34, 102, 117
Les Noces, 43, 46, 72, 109

Octuor, 39–40, 108
Oedipus Rex, 21–32, 44, 57, 97, 106–107, 135–144
L'Oiseau de feu, see *The Firebird*
Orpheus, 34, 54, 78

Pastorale, 134
Pater Noster, 26
Perséphone, 18, 34, 36–38, 42–43
Petrushka, 25, 53, 72, 104, 110
Piano Rag Music, 54
Plaisanteries musicales, 133
Polonaise from *Pan Voyevoda* (Rimsky-Korsakov, orch. I.S.), 133
Pulcinella, 34

Ragtime, 52, 54
The Rake's Progress, 22, 34, 67, 73, 108, 121
Renard, 40, 109

Requiem Canticles, 63, 70–71
Romances (Gorodetsky), see Two Melodies
Le Rossignol, see *The Nightingale*

Le Sacre du printemps, 41, 81–90, 105, 110
Scènes de Ballet, 42, 48–50
Scherzo à la russe, 52–53
Scherzo fantastique, 34, 115
A Sermon, a Narrative and a Prayer, 46, 110
The Soldier's Tale, see *Histoire du soldat*
Sonata for Piano (1904), 134
Sonata for Piano (1924), 26, 40, 106
Sonata for Two Pianos, 40, 42

Spring (*La Novice*), see Two Melodies
Symphony in E flat, 132, 134
Symphony in Three Movements, 50–52
Symphony of Psalms, 44–47

Three Pieces for Clarinet Solo, 54
Threni, 103
Two Melodies (Gorodetsky), 134
Two Songs of the Flea (Beethoven and Mussorgsky, orch. I.S.), 132

The Wedding, see *Les Noces*

Zvezdoliki, 121

INDEX OF PEOPLE AND PLACES

Alberti, Domenico, 27
Alfieri, Vittorio: *Memoirs*, 124
Amar, Licco, 102
Amsterdam, 102
Amy, Gilbert: *Antiphonies*, 59
Ansermet, Ernest, 54
Aron, André, 139
Arp, Jean, 16
Auden, W. H., 37, 92
Auerbach, Erich, 72

Babbitt, Milton: *The Widow's Lament in Springtime*, 100
Babin, Victor, 17
Bach, J. S., 30, 47, 56, 103, 121, 123–124, 127; *Aus der Tiefe* (Cantata No. 131), 94; Concerto for Two Violins, 47; 'Goldberg' Variations, 28; Two part Inventions, 40
Bach, C. P. E., 132
Baden-Baden (Germany), 43
Baird, Tadeusz: *Erotica*, 59
Balanchine, George, 37; *Apollon Musagète*, 33; *Balustrade*, 48; *Circus Polka*, 52–53; *The Flood*, 72–80; *A Midsummer Night's Dream*, 115
Barcelona, 47
Bauchant, André, 34
Baudelaire, Charles, 69
Beerbohm, Max, 95
Beethoven, Ludwig van, 30, 43, 112–117, 120, 124; Concerto for Violin, 47; 'Great Fugue,' 114, 124; Sonata in A-flat for Piano, 113; 'Song of the Flea' (Goethe), 132; String Quartets, 113–115, 124; Symphony No. 4, 112; Symphony No. 6 ('Pastoral'), 69; Symphony No. 8, 112; Symphony No. 9 ('Choral'), 112–114

Belaiev, Mitrofan, 134
Belline, Ira, 48
Belsky, Vladimir, 133
Bennett, Robert Russell, 50
Berg, Alban, 105, 120; Chamber Concerto, 100; *Lulu*, 100, 121; *Der Wein*, 105; *Wozzeck*, 124–125
Berlin, 14, 25, 48, 102, 104–105, 132
Bessie (circus elephant), 52–53
Bey, Tara, 95
Bible, The Holy, 44–46, 72, 131–132
Bizet, Georges: *Carmen*, 117–118
Blumenfeld, Felix, 134
Boethius, Manlius Severinus, 31
Boileau-Despréaux, Nicolas: *L'Art poétique*, 33
Bosset, Vera de, see Stravinsky, Vera
Boston (Massachusetts), 53
Boulanger, Nadia, 42
Boulez, Pierre, 59, 82–90, 105; *Structures*, 127
Brahms, Johannes, 30, 43, 89, 106, 126; Concerto for Violin, 47; Symphony No. 2, 115
Brancusi, Constantin, 112
Briand, Aristide, 98
Browning, E. B., 55
Brueghel, Pieter, 95
Brummell, Beau, 115
Buenos Aires, 43
Byron, Lord, 119

Carlyle, Thomas, 96
Carter, Elliott: Double Concerto, 99–101; Quartets Nos. 1 & 2, 100
Casella, Alfredo, 41
Catherwood, Frederick, 94
Celeste (I.S.'s cat), 14
Chaminade, Cécile, 119
Chanel, Gabrielle, 34, 140–141
Chaplin, Charles, 101
Charpentier, Gustave: *Louise*, 110
Charpentier, Marc-Antoine, 110
Chicago, 53
Chopin, Frederik, 115; *Valses*, 54
Christian, Charles, 53
Cicero, Marcus Tullius, 22, 31
Claudel, Paul, 36
Cocteau, Jean, 14, 17, 74, 97–98; *Antigone*, 22; *David*, 97; *Oedipus Rex* (lib. for I.S.), 21–23, 25, 29–30, 97, 135–138, 140–141, 144; *Orphée*, 97–98
Coleridge, S. T., 82, 129
Columbia (French gramophone company), 43
Coolidge, Elizabeth Sprague, 32
Copland, Aaron: *Twelve Poems of Emily Dickinson*, 100
Craft, Robert, 13–18, 21, 30, 32, 36, 39–40, 44, 47–48, 50, 52, 72–80, 82–90, 91, 97, 99, 101–102, 104, 107, 109, 112, 115, 117; *Expositions and Developments* (with I.S.), 133; *Memories and Commentaries* (with I.S.), 109, 134
Craig, Edward Gordon, 24

Dahl, Ingolf, 50
Daniélou, Alain, 30
Daniélou, Jean, 30; *Oedipus Rex* (tr. of Cocteau's lib.), 30–31; *Sacramentum Futuri*, 30
Dante Alighieri: *La Divina Commedia*, 65–66
Debussy, Claude, 58, 66, 109–110; *Clair de lune*, 34; *La Mer*, 78
Delibes, Léo, 33
Diaghilev, Serge, 17, 24–25, 32, 40–41, 97, 104, 138, 140–144

Dickinson, Emily, 67, 100
Dietrich, Marlene, 101
Disney, Walt, 126; *Fantasia*, 88
Dolin, Anton, 48–49
Dushkin, Samuel, 47

Echarvines les Bains (Dauphiné), 44
Ehrenzweig, Anton: *Psychoanalysis of Artistic Vision and Hearing*, 104
Eloy, Jean-Claude: *Equivalences*, 59
Emerson, Ralph Waldo, 66

Fairchild, Blair, 47
Flaubert, Gustave, 17, 27
Ford Foundation, 100
Francis of Assisi, St., 21–22, 26, 102
Franz Joseph, Emperor, 61
Freund, Marya, 106

Genoa, 21–22
Gershwin, George, 101–102; *Rhapsody in Blue*, 101
Giacometti, Alberto, 14
Gide, André, 36–37; *Anthologie de la poésie française* and *Perséphone*, 37
Giraudoux, Jean, 98; *Ondine*, 48
Glazunov, Alexander, 99, 131–132, 134; *Scènes de ballet*, 50
Gleason, Jackie, 17
Gnessin, Mikhail, 99
Goddard, Paulette, 101
Goethe, J. W. von, 128, 132; 'Song of the Flea,' 132
Gorodetsky, Sergei, 134
Goudimel, Claude, 110
Gounod, Charles, 117
Greenberg, Noah, 59
Gregory of Nyssa, St., 30
Grenoble, 47
Gretchaninov, Alexander, 99
Grofé, Ferde, 58
Guézec, *Architectures colorées*, 59
Gurian (galosh merchant), 46

Hamburg, 14
Handel, G. F., 25
Haydn, Joseph, 30; 'Military' Symphony, 111

Heard, Gerald, 91–93
Henze, Hans Werner: *Boulevard Solitude*, 102
Herman, Woody, 53
Herriot, Edouard, 58
Heurtebise (lift company), 97–98
Heyworth, Peter, 131
Hindemith, Paul, 25, 102–103
Hofmannsthal, Hugo von, 48
Hollywood, 13, 16–17, 49, 72, 91–94, 96, 101, 106
Homburg-vor-der-Höhe (Germany), 116
Horapollo (Horus Apollo): *Hieroglyphica*, 48
Hubble, Edwin, 95
Hudson, Rock, 103
Hurok, Sol, 17, 48
Hutchins, Robert, 95
Huxley, Aldous, 14, 91–92, 94–97
Huxley, Julian, 94
Huxley, Maria, 96

Indy, Vincent d', 110
Ingegneri, Marc-Antonio, 110
Isherwood, Christopher, 91–94, 102
Iturbi, José, 42
Ives, Charles, 66–67; Symphonies Nos. 3 and 4 and *Three Places in New England*, 66

Jeffrey, Francis, 96
John XXIII, Pope, 13
John of the Cross, St., 129
Jones, Robert Edmond, 24
Josquin des Prés: *Hic Me Sidereo*, 124
Joyce, James: *Ulysses*, 59

Kandinsky, Vasily, 120
Karajan, Herbert von, 82–90, 121
Kennedy, John Fitzgerald, 14, 68
Khrushchev, Nikita, 56
Klemperer, Otto, 25, 103, 106
Kochanski, Paul, 101
Kokoschka, Oskar, 103
Koni, Anatol: *Vospominaniya O Pisatiliach*, 70
Křenek, Ernst, 102–104; *Jonny Spielt Auf*, *Lamentations of Jeremiah*, *Spiritus Intelligentiae Sanctus*, *Studies in Counterpoint* and *Symphonic Elegy*, 103
Kusmin, Mikhail, 41
Kuznetzov, Maria *et fils*, 132

Lang, Paul Henry, 71
Lausanne (Switzerland), 42
Lawrence, D. H., 96
Lecocq, Charles, 117; *Le Coeur à la main* and *Giroflé, Girofla*, 117
Leningrad (=St. Petersburg, = Petrograd), 41, 46, 99, 104, 106, 115–117, 121, 131–132
Lessing, Gotthold Ephraim, 14
Lévi-Strauss, Claude, 69–70
Lewis, C. S., 36
Leysin (Switzerland), 97
Liberace, 123
Lifar, Serge, 33
Lombardo, Guy, 118
London, 43, 94, 97, 111
Lorenz, Konrad, 58
Los Angeles, 53, 55, 95, 103–104, 106
Louis XIV, King, 34
Lourdes (France), 125
Lzy (Russia), 133

McLuhan, Marshall, 64–66
Magaloff, Nikita, 17
Mahler, Gustav, 30, 106
Mahler-Werfel, Alma, 106
Malraux, André, 59
Marcus, Adele, 43
Markova, Alicia, 48–49
Marseilles, 37
Maupassant, Guy de, 17
Maurois, André, 93
Melbourne (Australia), 131
Mendelssohn-Bartholdy, Felix, 114–115; *The Fair Melusine*, *A Midsummer Night's Dream* (overture and incidental music), Octet, *Rondo Capriccioso*, String Symphony No. 9 and Symphony No. 4 ('Italian'), 115
Messager, André, 117

Messiaen, Olivier, 59, 69; *Chronochromie* and *La Rousserolle effarvatte*, 59
Meyerbeer, Giacomo, 25
Milan, 41
Milhaud, Darius, 42, 106
Mill, John Stuart, 94
Minkowski, Hermann, 39
Mitussov, Stepan, 133
Monte Carlo, 141
Monteux, Pierre, 117
Morand, Paul, 98
Morges (Switzerland), 40–41, 54, 106
Moscow, 60, 99, 117
Mozart, Wolfgang Amadeus, 30, 116, 121; *Don Giovanni*, 23; Fugue in C minor, 43; *Requiem*, 63; the violin concerti, 47
Muncie (Indiana), 67
Munich, 51, 82, 103
Mussorgsky, Modest: 'Song of the Flea' (Goethe), 132

Naples, 41
New Orleans, 53
New York, 24, 50, 53, 91, 101–102, 132
Nice, 21–22, 26, 44, 47, 103, 135, 138–144
Nono, Luigi, 56
Norton, Charles Eliot, 104
Nouvel, Walter, 41, 141, 143–144

Oberlin (Ohio), 57
Ocampo, Victoria, 94
Ockeghem, Johannes, 103
Offenbach, Jacques, 103

Paestum (Italy), 102
Pareto, Vilfredo, 80
Paris, 15–16, 25, 32, 36, 38, 40–41, 43, 50, 54, 97–98, 101–102, 106–107, 139–144
Parker, Charlie, 53
Pascal, Blaise, 41
Perse, St.-John, 22, 97–98; *Pour fêter une enfance*, 98

Philadelphia, 50
Philo Judaeus, 30
Piaf, Edith, 117
Picasso, Pablo, 54, 97
Pleyel Company, 42–43, 54
Polignac, Prince and Princess Edmond de, 25, 36, 138, 141
Porter, Cole, 50
Positano (Italy), 102
Prague, 115
Psellus Akritas: *De Ceremoniis*, 123
Puccini, Giacomo: *La Bohème*, *La Fanciulla del West* and *Madama Butterfly*, 58
Pushkin, Alexander, 33

Racine, Jean: *Phèdre*, 22, 34
Ravel, Maurice, 41, 101
Rebikov, Vladimir, 99; *Yelka*, 99
Redon, Odilon, 34
Reinhardt, Werner, 42
Renan, Ernest, 129
Richter, Nicolas, 133–134
Riga (Latvia), 142–143
Rimbaud, Arthur, 98, 119
Rimsky-Korsakov, Nicolai, 41, 99, 117; *Pan Voyevoda*, 133; *The Tableau of Tsar Saltan*, 134; wife (Nadejda), 133
Ringling Brothers' Circus, 53
Robbins Landon, H. C.: *Supplement to the Symphonies of Joseph Haydn*, 111
Robinson, Edward G., 101
Rome (Italy), 24
Rosario (Argentina), 43
Rosbaud, Hans, 107
Rose, Billy, 48, 50; *The Seven Lively Arts*, 50
Roslavetz, Nicolai, 99; Three Compositions for Piano, 99
Rossini, Gioacchino, 18
Roussel, Albert, 110
Rubinstein, Artur, 92
Rubinstein, Ida, 36
Ruggles, Carl: *Angels* and *Lilacs*, 100
Ryle, Gilbert, 116

Saint-Exupéry, Antoine de, 55
St. Petersburg, see Leningrad
Saint-Saëns, Camille, 35, 86
San Diego (California), 95
Santa Fe (New Mexico), 58, 103
Santa Monica (California), 93
Sarasota (Florida), 53
Sargent, Winthrop, 71
Satie, Erik, 41
Schall, Eric, 51
Scherchen, Hermann, 16, 105
Schlegel, August Wilhelm, 115
Schnabel, Artur, 131-132; Cello Sonata and *Duodecimet*, 132; *My Life and Music*, 131
Schoenberg, Arnold, 25, 30, 90, 99, 102-109, 111, 115, 119-121, 129, 132; *Erwartung*, 22, 105-106; Five Pieces for Orchestra, 105; Four Orchestral Songs, 60, 111; *Die glückliche Hand*, 60, 105, 109; *Die Jakobsleiter*, 59-61, 109; *Kammersymphonie*, 99, 106; *Moses und Aron*, 107, 109, 121; *Pelleas und Melisande*, 106; *Pierrot lunaire*, 104-106, 120; Prelude to *Genesis*, 106, 108; Septet-Suite, 106; 'Seraphita', see Four Orchestral Songs; Serenade, 106; Six Pieces for Male Chorus, 108; String Quartet No. 4, 108; String Trio, 114; *A Survivor from Warsaw*, 108; *Verklärte Nacht*, 104, 108; Violin Concerto, 47; first wife (Mathilde), 104
Schott (music publishers), 102
Schubert, Franz, 30, 114-116; *Gretchen am Spinnrade*, 54; *Marche militaire*, 53; Symphonies Nos. 4 and 8 ('Unfinished'), 116
Schumann, Clara, 116
Schumann, Robert, 54, 114-117; Symphony No. 4, 116-117
Schütz, Heinrich: *Requiem*, 71
Semov, 93
Sessions, Roger: *Idyll of Theocritus*, 100
Shakespeare, William: *King Lear*, 71; *A Midsummer Night's Dream*, 155

Shilkret, Nathaniel (*et al.*): *Genesis Suite*, 106
Siloti, Alexander, 132; *Vospominaniya i Pisina*, 104
Sophocles, 128; *Oedipus Rex*, 22-23, 28-29
Spenser, Edmund, 27
Spiegelman, Joel, 17
Stalin, Josef, 56
Steegmuller, Francis: *Flaubert and Madame Bovary* and *Maupassant*, 17
Steinberg, Maximilian, 99, 134
Stendhal (Henri Beyle), 95
Stern, Issac, 17
Steuermann, Eduard, 105
Stockhausen, Karlheinz, 127; *Momente*, 127
Stokowski, Leopold, 121
Strauss, Johann, 103
Strauss, Richard, 48, 66, 106; *Four Last Songs*, 71; *Salome*, 85
THE STRAVINSKY FAMILY
Anna (I.S.'s mother), 48
Catherine (I.S.'s first wife, Catherine Nossenko), 21, 97, 138
Feodor (I.S.'s father), 99, 116, 126, 131
Ignace Ignatievich (I.S.'s great-grandfather), 63
Igor, *passim*; see Index of Works by Stravinsky for compositions mentioned in the text
Ludmila (=Mika, I.S.'s elder daughter), 41, 43
Maria Milena (I.S.'s younger daughter), 15, 43
Sviatoslav Soulima (I.S.'s younger son), 42-43, 132
Theodore (I.S.'s elder son), 41, 43, 140-141, 144
Vera (I.S.'s second wife, Vera de Bosset), 17, 38, 40-41, 43, 51; intro. to her paintings by A. Huxley, 96-97
Strawson, P. F.: *Individuals*, 109
Strecker, Willy, 47, 102
Suvchinsky, Pierre, 36
Swift, Jonathan: *Gulliver's Travels*, 62

Tatum, Art, 53
Tchaikovsky, Peter Ilyich, 27, 33, 114, 117; *Pique-Dame*, 117; *Swan Lake*, 116
Tchelitchev, Pavel, 37, 48, 73; designs for *Apollo*, *Balustrade* and *Ondine*, 48
Tcherepnin, Nicolai, 99, 132
Tchernigov (Russia), 99
Thévenaz, Paulet, 97
Thoreau, Henry David: *Walden*, 67
Tiflis (Russia), 59
Tolstoy, Alexei Konstantinovich: *Koosma Prootkov* (with Jemchooshnikov bros.), 134
Tolstoy, Leo, 70; *Resurrection*, 94
Totnes (Devon), 94
Toumanova, Tamara, 48
Toynbee, Arnold: *A Study of History*, 128–129
Trakl, Georg, 103
Tuckerman, Frederick, 67

Ussachevsky, Vladimir, 17
Utrillo, Maurice, 15

Van Eyck, Jan, 59
Van Gogh, Vincent, 15
Varèse, Edgar, 109–112; *Amériques*, 109–110, 112; *Arcana*, 109–110, 112; *Density 21.5*, 109; *Déserts*, 109–112; *Ecuatorial*, 109; *Ionisation*, 111; *Nocturnal*, 112; *Offrandes* ('Chanson de là-haut' and 'La Croix du sud'), 110, 112
Veblen, Thorstein, 57
Vehchasha (Russia), 133
Venice, 21, 26, 56, 105–106
Verdi, Giuseppe, 27, 113; *La Forza del Destino*, 37; *Rigoletto*, 79; *Il Trovatore*, 34

Vienna, 25, 106
Villefranche (France), 135–137
Voltaire, François-Marie Arouet de, 128
Voreppe (Grenoble), 42, 47, 135
Vronsky, Vitya, 17

Wagner, Richard, 27, 30, 89, 106; *Die Meistersinger*, 29; *Der Ring des Nibelungen*, 75
Waley, Arthur, 94
Walpole, Horace, 91
Washington, D.C., 25, 32, 98
Waugh, Evelyn, 14, 91–92; *The Loved One*, 91
Weber, Carl Maria von, 115; *Der Freischütz*, *Invitation to the Dance* and *Konzertstück*, 115
Webern, Anton, 105, 109, 111, 124
Wellesz, Egon, 45
Werfel, Franz, 37
Whiteman, Paul, 53
Whitman, Walt, 67
Widor, Charles-Marie, 110
Wilde, Oscar, 37
Wilson, Sandy: *The Boy Friend*, 36
Wolpe, Stefan: Symphony, 100
Worcester (Massachusetts), 43

Xenakis, Yannis, 126

Yastrebtzev, V.: *Recollections of Rimsky-Korsakov*, 133–134
Yukawa, Hideki, 65

Zehme, Albertine, 104
Zemlinsky, Alexander von, 115
Zeretelli, Prince A., 139, 142–143
Zillig, Winfried, 60
Zorina, Vera, 37, 52–53